D0437865

'No Fine on Fun'

'No Fine on Fun'

THE COMICAL HISTORY OF THE
ENTERTAINMENTS DUTY

BY

A. P. HERBERT

METHUEN & COMPANY LTD
36 ESSEX STREET · STRAND · LONDON W.C.2

FIRST PUBLISHED IN 1957

CATALOGUE NO. 5970/U
PRINTED IN GREAT BRITAIN BY
THE CAMELOT PRESS LTD
LONDON AND SOUTHAMPTON

With due salutes
to
The Right Honourable
HAROLD MACMILLAN
A
humble contribution
to his
Inquiry

Acknowledgments

I have to thank the Controller of Her Majesty's Stationery Office for his permission to make some extracts from the Official Report (House of Commons).

I thank, too, Mr Roger Morgan of the House of Commons Library, Commander Christopher Powell, R.N., secretary to the Theatres Entertainment Tax Committee, the President (Mr S. E. Linnit) and assistant secretary (Mr G. Robinson) of the Society of West End Theatre Managers, Sir Stanley Rous, secretary to the Football Association, Mr Ellis F. Pinkney, M.C., secretary to the Cinematograph Exhibitors Association of Great Britain and Ireland, Mr Frederic Carter of Associated Theatre Properties, Mr Peter Saunders, Miss E. M. Barber, secretary to the League of Dramatists, and the British Drama League, for information and assistance; and

My excellent secretary, Mrs Judy-Jane Hargreaves, for her devoted, careful, and exhausting labours.

A.P.H.

Introduction

HERE is the comical history of the Entertainments Duty: and, to those not seriously affected, some of it may be extremely funny. Where it is not, you may still be interested in the ins and outs of a Parliamentary battle which has lasted for forty years. Indeed, the serious student of our Parliamentary system, of the power of the Civil Service (especially the Treasury) and the impotence of the 'sovereign Parliament' in financial affairs, should not miss a word. It should be a 'lesson' to the House of Commons too—never to let the Treasury have a bad tax because of an 'emergency', or, if they must, to put a stern time-limit in the Act. Here is an accident of war which, like some concrete 'strong-point' on the banks of the Upper Thames, seems, forty years after, to be acquiring permanency. Parliament after Parliament has vigorously attacked it. Chancellor after Chancellor, hard-pressed in debate, has confessed his dislike or discontent. Several have promised to 'remodel' it: four or five, to their credit, have hacked small corners off it; others have added adornments, urged on by a school of thought which finds the ruin not merely useful but admirable. Twenty years ago, on a free vote of the House of Commons, the tax on the theatre, at least, could have been abolished. Time and again, between three and four hundred Members, of all the Parties, have put their names to that impious suggestion. But the tenacity of the Treasury, the discipline of the Whips, with, now and then, the timely aid of war or 'crisis', have preserved it: and here it is today, chipped and cracked but wrapped in ivy, almost an 'ancient monument'. You must admire, at least, the industry and pertinacity of your Members, though you need not read all the speeches I have quoted. Here and there we may have repeated ourselves; but so did the Ministers: and to make an impression on the Treasury you must use the patience and the power of water dripping on stone. The length and strength of the struggle, I feel, are a kind of evidence of good character. No one now suggests the abolition of the income tax, or the tax on whisky or tobacco, though we may complain that they are too high. But this rebellion gains power through the years, and will not be put down. One day, I am sure, the whole tax will be swept away, for the same reason that we rejected the tax on newspapers and books, not because it makes men poorer but because it is uncivilized.

But that day is not yet. High hopes, which I share, were raised by the speech of Mr Harold Macmillan, Chancellor of the Exchequer, in the House of Commons on 26 June 1956. But high hopes have been raised by Chancellors before: and then, the next year, have been cast down by foreign or financial trouble. I should not like to bet that Parliament will not have to fight the same old battles again—even about the theatre—in 1957 and the years beyond. Those outside may well, this year at least, be tempted to relax, and to spare themselves their annual labours, the conferences, the anxious decisions, the drafting, the deputations. But the forces against them will be as strong as ever: and so I hope that this account may help to keep their battle alive. Here is all the ammunition in a single store—at least, I cannot think of any argument, on either side, that does not somewhere appear in these pages. My chief brief has always been for the theatre, and so long as the tax remains, it must be. But I feel for all the victims of this impost. I have told their tale as well, and have outlined the latest case for the cinema and football, for example. I have perhaps done too much, for my own good, in this good cause, and can do no more. But I leave this story as my last offering to the people of the theatre, and to all the other makers and merchants of fine art or 'fun' who may have to carry on the fight.

14 *July* 1956

Sundry Sayings

'The tax was put on designedly to make substantial contributions towards the war from those who are not hit, or are not hit so directly, by other direct taxes.'

Mr Montagu, Financial Secretary to the Treasury, 1916

'The Chancellor of the Exchequer, in 1916, assured the Football Association that this was only an emergency measure.'

Football Association, 1956

'Some restraint should be placed on the expenditure of money on amusements of this kind during a time of war.'

Mr Fell, M.P., 1916

'I have no sympathy whatsoever with the cinema entertainments.'

Mr T. M. Healy, M.P., 1916

'I dislike this tax in principle.'

Mr Philip Snowden, Chancellor of the Exchequer, 1926

'I shall be glad, if my resources enable me, to remodel the whole tax, because I think that in its present form it is unsatisfactory, both theoretically and practically.'

Mr Neville Chamberlain, Chancellor of the Exchequer, 1934

'I conceive that "education", for the statesman, should embrace the whole wide world of mental enrichment, including literature, art and music, the "wireless", the press, and what is loosely called "entertainment". In this wide field I think that the State is lamentably idle and unhelpful. It is absurd with one hand to distribute free education and with the other to lay a punitive tax upon the drama, concerts, and the takings of the B.B.C. The Entertainment Duty (a tax of 15 per cent on receipts not profits) is a barbarous relic of the Great War. It couples blindly the plays of Shakespeare and the exhibition of performing seals. . . . Admitting the imperfections of much public entertainment, I regard it as a tax upon knowledge and enlightenment and the free communication of minds. I shall therefore press for its abolition, at least, where it is imposed upon music and the living theatre.'

Letter to the Electors of Oxford University,
A. P. Herbert, 1935

'I do share a great deal of the feeling against this particular form of tax. . . . I will during the year have the working of these taxes studied. . . . Really and truly, in this country, the ancient home of culture and art and literature, this tax ought not to be allowed automatically to continue without very serious examination.'

Sir John Simon, Chancellor of the Exchequer, 1938

'I hope conditions may be such that in due course we may be able to mitigate taxes of this kind, because it is a matter of regret that the theatre, particularly, should be affected in this way.'

Sir Kingsley Wood, Chancellor of the Exchequer, 1940

'I cannot accept the contention that the printed word should necessarily be immune from taxation . . . but I think that, on the whole, I should agree that books, as well as newspapers, should be exempt from the tax—at least for the present.'

Sir Kingsley Wood, Chancellor of the Exchequer, 1940

'If it were an easier time and I found it possible to distribute some more revenue by way of tax reduction, I am sure that the living theatre would stand high on the list. . . .

What I should like to do would be to have a discussion between now and next year. . . .'

Dr Dalton, Chancellor of the Exchequer, 1947

'Dr. Dalton instituted an inquiry . . . I readjusted the tax on lines which were in response to the inquiry. . . . Hence the new Entertainments Duty Structure. . . .'

Mr R. A. Butler, Chancellor of the Exchequer, 1953

'We have set on foot a thorough-going review of all sections of the Entertainments Duty.'

Mr H. Brooke, Financial Secretary to the Treasury, 1956

'I will look very carefully at the structure of Entertainments Duty as a whole. . . . When the time comes, as I believe it may well come next year, for making relaxations . . . I give this pledge, and I state it quite deliberately. I hope that this will be the last occasion on which it will be necessary for me or for Treasury Ministers to defend the tax upon the living theatre, or indeed the Entertainments Duty in its present form.'

Mr Harold Macmillan, Chancellor of the Exchequer, 1956

'I offer to all parties this battle-cry: "No Tax on Thought—No Duty on Beauty—No Levy on Laughter—and No Fine on Fun!" '

Speech at the Academy Dinner, 1953, A. P. Herbert

I

Birth and Early Life

[1]

THE tax on drama, music, films, football, racing, etc., was invented by some sour Treasury fellow in the First World War and made its ugly bow in the Finance (New Duties) Bill, 1916.[1] The other new duties were on matches, cider, perry, soda-water-siphons, and, believe it or not, on railway fares over 9*d.*—a queer collection. The railways were then 'private enterprise'; they had directors in the House, and it needs no genius to guess that the railway-ticket tax was never carried. After the war most of the other duties departed too. Matches came back—I cannot say when—and cider came back in 1956. But drama, music, etc., have remained till today, and are still taxed as if they were Red Biddy or cancer-causing cigarettes—though not so much.

1916. A 'TEMPORARY' TAX

This is odd. For the tale is, and the Treasury have never contradicted it,[2] that in the spring of 1916 the Chancellor of the Exchequer, Mr Reginald McKenna, summoned the theatrical managers to the Treasury and said: 'Don't make

[1] Rate (1916): 1*s.* + 2*d.*; 6*s.* + 6*d.*; 10*s.* 6*d.* + 1*s.*; 12*s.* 6*d.* + 1*s.*

[2] I told it myself in the House of Commons, *Hansard*, Vol. 424, col. 264, 19 June 1946, also in *The Times*, and there was not the slightest attempt to deny it. The Football Association, they say, received the same assurance.

a fuss, dear boys. This is a temporary tax. It will be abolished, I promise you' (big laugh coming) 'as soon as the war is won.' The story at least explains the statement made by Mr Montagu, for the Government, in the House. 'We appreciate the welcome which this tax has received from those who are connected with the theatrical and entertainment circles. They have not resented in any way the imposition of the tax. I think that they have received it in a cheerful spirit.' (*Hansard*, Vol. 81, col. 1849.)

Speeches in the House clearly show that it was considered as a war-tax. With the other 'niggling little duties' (Mr Hogge), it was 'put on designedly to take substantial contributions towards the War from those who are not hit, or are not so directly, by other direct taxes' (Mr Montagu).

'... The whole design of this tax is not to prevent people going either to the cinema or the theatre, but to make them pay some contribution to the war when they go. It is one of the least wasteful forms of expenditure. It does not consume much labour, and it does not consume any commodity; therefore I should be very sorry to drive anybody to the consumption of sweets or alcohol rather than to go to these amusements ...' (Mr Montagu, Vol. 81, col. 1542)

But here and there, as well, a faintly moral note was sounded. 'People who visit places of amusement *at a time like this* ought to be made to contribute to the War. I do not think anyone would object to that.' (Mr Lough) 'Some restraint should be placed on the expenditure of money on amusements of this kind during a time of war.' (Mr Fell) (All this is queer reading for anyone who remembers what praise the theatres received—in both Great Wars—for their contributions to 'morale'.) In such an atmosphere was the tax conceived, of wartime panic, prejudice, and ignorance. The date imaginatively named for the first collection of the first tax on Old England's 'amusements' was May Day.

THE PICTURE PALACE

The main target was that new monster, the cinema. 'The great source of revenue,' said the Chancellor, 'will be the cinema picture palaces.' Members did not think much of them. 'I have no sympathy whatsoever with the cinema entertainments,' said Mr T. M. Healy. Mr Lough, in a charming passage, said: 'If somebody pays *2d.* for admission to one of these questionable forms of entertainment—I have never seen one of these picture entertainments—(An HON. MEMBER: "Why questionable?")—I withdraw the word "questionable" if it is objected to . . .'

Mr Hogge justly complained: 'This tax seems to be regarded entirely from the point of view of the cinema theatres. We must bear in mind that there are other places of amusement and in particular the theatres, which are also involved in this tax . . .' But the theatre was hardly ever mentioned.

Mr Hogge said, too:

'. . . . Apparently the most popular tax of all is that which is to be put on amusements. Everybody seems to think that will be a tremendously productive tax, and that the right thing is to tax the amusements of the people. I differ absolutely and entirely from that line and the basis on which the tax has presumably been put. . . .

'. . . My general view is that I do not think it is a wise thing to tax the cheap entertainment because of the effect it has had on the people. I think it is a contributory cause to the increasing sobriety of the people of this country. I think it is a great pity that the burden of this tax should be brought down on the people who until those amusements were created had not the opportunity of an outlet for relief from the routine and drab monotony of their lives . . .

'. . . it is a war effort and the money must be raised on account of the War, but let us in doing that try to do as little injustice as possible . . .' (cols. 1557-61)

The voice of sense and civilization was heard, as well, from Mr David Mason: 'What is one man's amusement may not be another man's amusement, and it is grossly unfair that you should introduce this pettifogging method of raising taxation by imposing it on the man who gets his recreation by going to a music-hall entertainment or a cinema exhibition and not impose a similar burden on the man who secures his recreation by reading books . . .'. Today he might have added 'or listening to the radio'. But in those days—imagine it!—the B.B.C. did not exist.

The estimated yield of the tax, picture palaces and all, was a mere £5,000,000. Russia, it was said, had a similar tax—levied at 10 per cent—and Sir J. D. Rees advised the Chancellor to consult the Russian Ambassador about the details.

On 12 April 1916, in Committee on the Bill, Clause 3 (Railway Fares) was withdrawn. Mr Butcher had moved an amendment to exempt 'commercial travellers'. Mr Montagu said that the Government had been so moved by this and other 'difficulties'—'these undoubted hardships'—and the loss of revenue which would be suffered if they were met, that it was 'not worthwhile to ask the Committee to go further in the matter. It is with considerable reluctance that the Government gives up £3,000,000 of revenue, but the tax would have to be so *mutilated* as to be not worth the trouble of collecting.'

The tax on Tschaikowsky, films, football, etc., remained. It has been so 'mutilated' that the tax on the living theatre yields less than £2,000,000 today. But it remains.

[2]

EXEMPTIONS, ETC.

Clearly, a good job was not done in 1916: for Parliament has tinkered with the tax in 1917, 1918, 1919, 1921, 1922, 1923, 1924, 1931, 1935, 1940, 1942, 1943, 1946, 1947, 1948, 1949, 1950, 1952, 1953, and 1954, not to mention the Entertainments Duty Regulations of 1955: and even that list, I believe, is not exhaustive.

The *Encyclopaedia Britannica* speaks of 'the taxation of luxuries': but from the first, it is clear, the Treasury had a faintly guilty conscience. It agreed that not every 'entertainment' could be accounted criminal, even in time of war. So an entertainment 'of a wholly educational character' was exempt—and this is still the law; also, as a rule, what was not done for the beastly purpose of profit. It was when what might be 'educational' was done for 'profit' that confusion crept in, and they are in precisely the same muddle today. I often urged the late Sir Charles Cochran to refuse to pay the tax on the ground that one of his productions was 'wholly educational'. In a court of law I think he might have won: unfortunately, under the Act, the final arbiter is the Minister of Education. 'Where', said Mr David Mason in the House on 12 April 1916, 'are you to draw the line between what is educational and what is amusing? The difficulties will be endless.' A High Court Judge said much the same thing on the Bench in May 1956.

The duty is not charged when the 'entertainment' is provided by a school not conducted for 'profit': nor where it is provided for educational or scientific purposes by a society not seeking to make a profit, or with the object of reviving national pastimes: nor is it charged in respect of entertainments consisting solely of the products of an industry, a display of skill by workmen in an industry, or works of graphic art, sculpture and arts craftsmanship, executed and exhibited by persons who practise graphic art, sculpture or 'arts craftsmanship' *for profit* and as their main occupation; or of displays of skill by such persons in such arts and crafts.

All this rigmarole is taken from the original Act, and is still the law, except that 'exhibitions', as above, now have to be 'not for profit'.

At the last minute, on the Report stage, a special paragraph was added for the protection of such 'entertainments' as the Zoo. This, without the intention of the Founders, has been causing trouble in the theatre for 20 years (see IV—1946).

Why, you may ask, all this twittering about 'profit'? As we have seen, in 1916 it was considered unworthy to be 'amused' in time of war, and worse, it follows, to amuse others for profit; and, in time of peace, one can understand a good Socialist singing this song. But is it not strange that for forty years Conservative administrations have maintained a tax which is governed and engined by an antipathy to 'profit'? There is no tax on admission to the Royal Academy Summer Exhibition, for pictures are educational and the Society does not 'seek to make a profit', though the artists do. But if one of the same artists has an exhibition at the Galleries of Mr Brown, who has to pay rent and makes a small charge for admission, Entertainment Tax is payable.[1] Does this make sense? No statesman complains if a publisher seeks to make a profit—peace or war.

The exemptions and compromises in the Act were not enough. They have been growing like an ugly rash all over it, and now there are 12 (or 13) classes of exemption, clearly but laughably set out in Notice 100 by the Commissioners of Customs and Excise.[2] There have been to date 12 changes of 'rate' on the living theatre alone, and there are now three different rates or 'scales' of duty (1) living theatre, etc., (2) sport, and (3) cinema.[3] There are some fascinating little problems where categories of entertainment or exemption overlap. What tax is payable, for example, where 'a flower show includes a vocal concert'—or 'an organist accompanies a silent film'? The flower show, if provided by a society not established for profit, would normally be exempt (under Section 11, Finance Act, 1923). But the 'vocal concert' would probably put it into the wicked amusements class, and it would be taxed under Scale 1. The organist and the silent film are more difficult.

[1] If the charge is more than 1*s*.

[2] See page 101. [3] See page 92.

But I *think* that, if the organist played for 'not less than one-quarter of the total time', the tax would be payable 'at a composite rate', that is, two-thirds of the duty chargeable on a film (Scale 3) plus one-third of the duty chargeable on the organist under Scale 1. Isn't it fun?

[3]

METHOD OF COLLECTION

The original intention, as we have seen, was that wretched citizens who saw fit to attend 'amusements' in time of war should make a special contribution to the cost of war. The original arrangements for collection conformed. Where there were no turnstiles recording automatically the number of persons 'paying for admission' stamps were to be affixed to every ticket sold.[1] This is still part of the official machinery. 'Proprietors' who do not care to provide their own tickets may secure from the Commissioners of Customs and Excise rolls of 'Government tickets' in distinctive and delightful colour schemes, thus:

Price of admission (including duty)	Duty value of ticket	Rolls (1000 tickets each)
At a sporting entertainment		
s. d.	s. d.	
3 0	0 8	Pink and yellow
3 6	0 10	Green and yellow
Or, at the cinema		
2 8	1 0	White and yellow
3 0	1 1¾	Blue and white

But at the theatre, and other entertainments where there are no turnstiles, the business of affixing stamps to tickets

[1] 'In so far as entry to amusements is obtained by tickets the matter is simple' (!) 'There will be a stamp on the tickets. It will be made illegal to issue a ticket which does not bear a stamp.' (Mr. Montagu, 4 April 1916, Vol. 81, col. 1157.)

would have been intolerably tiresome, not only to the 'proprietors' but to the taxing-authority. (I still hold to a private belief that the theatres, if they chose, could insist on a number of Customs men attending every night and affixing the stamps themselves: but I may be wrong, and, if I am right, nobody will try it.) Regulation 6 says that the proprietor shall (*a*) collect each stamped ticket and 'tear it into two parts across any stamp thereon', and (*b*) immediately return one part to the person from whom it was collected, and (*c*) retain the other part—and shall 'keep them until noon of the day after that on which they were collected unless they are earlier removed by an officer of Customs and Excise'.

Rather than do this dreadful drill, all concerned agreed, on the Report stage of the Bill, to what are called 'approved arrangements'. The stamp drill was not to be required when 'the proprietor of the entertainment has made arrangements approved by the Commissioners for furnishing returns of the payments for admission to the entertainment and has given security to an amount and in a manner approved by the Commissioners for the payment of duty'.

Thus the theatres, rather feebly, I feel, consented to act as tax-collectors, or, as Sir George Cave put it, "will be responsible for the whole of the duty', and, what is more, have to put down a sum of money as earnest that they will do the Government's job faithfully and well.

This was agreed to without a Division. But Members soon perceived that they were shifting the incidence of the tax. 'It would inevitably mean', said Sir T. Walters, 'that the proprietors would have to pay the tax sooner or later.' 'If you will allow this Amendment to stand', said Mr Hogge, 'there is nothing to prevent the proprietors of large and wealthy houses paying the tax themselves out of their receipts, without any charge to the people who come into their theatres.' The "smaller houses", he thought, would not be able to do this and so would be squeezed out. (17 April 1916, col. 2126.)

Mr J. Samuel said: 'It was intended, as the Clause was originally drafted, that each individual person should pay the duty, but now . . . the proprietor can forward returns to the Commissioners, and the probability is that no tax may be charged on the individual paying for admission. The owner may be wealthy enough to pay the tax himself.' (col. 2129.)

Sir George Cave, for the Government, said: 'We are told that the big proprietors will pay the duty themselves, but that the small proprietors cannot do it. But the desire is that both shall pass it on to the customer, and if it is not passed on then it must be shown on the ticket or notice how much of the price charged is payable on tax, so that the customer may know how much he is actually paying for the entertainment itself.'

Whatever happened forty years ago, there is no doubt that the 'proprietor' is 'paying the tax' today, not because he is 'wealthy', but because he cannot help it.

The tiresome question, 'Who pays—now?' is considered later. But, for the moment, the picture is very clearly shown by the official tables of 'rates', which are headed thus:

Charge to Public up to:	*Duty*	*Amount retained by Proprietor*
10*s.* 0*d.*	1*s.* 5½*d.*	8*s.* 6½*d.*

The manager pays—and the author too.[1]

In 1917 the rate was, for the most part, doubled.[2]

[1] See Appendix 'A'

[2] Rate (1917): 1*s.* + 3*d.*; 6*s.* + 1*s.*; 10*s.* 6*d.* + 1*s.* 6*d.*; 12*s.* 6*d.* + 2*s.*

II

After the (First) War

1920–1935

As soon as it was decent after the war, that is, in 1920, the theatre began its almost annual attempts to show that its 'welcome' in 1916 had not been given to a permanent tax. In 1919 the rate was slightly reduced on the 4*d.*–7*d.* seats.

In 1920, in Committee on the Finance Bill, Mr Newbold proposed a reduction in the rate of the duty (in effect from 1*s.* 3*d.* out of 6*s.* received to 1*s.*) and Mr Seddon, who seconded the amendment, said: '*My wish is to call the attention of the Chancellor of the Exchequer to the fact that this duty was originally a war measure.*'

The amendment was defeated by 135 votes to 9. Sir Robert Horne (the Chancellor) made no reply to Mr Seddon's point. (*Hansard*, 21 June 1920, cols. 1273–5.)

In 1921, the theatrical managers led a deputation to the Chancellor, who said that he 'could not afford' a reduction. In 1922 was formed a joint body representing all theatrical interests—the Stage and Allied Arts League.

In 1924 (MR PHILIP SNOWDEN) there was a new scale of duty—reducing the rate on payments up to 1*s.* 3*d.*[1] In 1926, 1927, and 1928 Mr Day (Labour) asked for more—in vain. But in 1926 MR SNOWDEN said that he disliked the duty in principle and, 'when the money was available' (the old, old story) he would like to relieve the dearer seats in the theatre as well.

[1] Rate (1924): 1*s.* + 2*d.*; 6*s.* + 1*s.*; 10*s.* 6*d.* + 1*s.* 6*d.*; 12*s.* 6*d.* + 2*s.*

In 1931 the rate was raised again.[1]

In 1932 the Sunday Entertainments Act was passed, which enabled the cinemas to open on Sundays—though with some hypocritical provisos about contributions to charity. The living theatre was excluded.

In 1933 Mr Alfred Denville, a lively man of the theatre himself, made what was, I believe, the first motion to get the tax abolished on the living theatre. Today, at last, in 1956, Mr Harold Macmillan, it seems, is thinking about this too: but it has taken 23 years to get the Treasury as far as that. Mr Hore-Belisha said kindly that 'No manipulation of the Entertainments Duty could compel people to see bad plays. Cinemas might have taken much of the public from the theatre, but that was hardly the fault of the duty.' O Lord, how many Financial Secretaries since then have been briefed by the Treasury to utter such unhelpful foolishness! It is like hitting a cripple on the head and saying 'Don't complain. This is by no means your only trouble'.

1935

MR NEVILLE CHAMBERLAIN

Mr Chamberlain, Chancellor of the Exchequer, thought that it was quite sensible to lay some blame on the Duty. The Fathers of the Act in 1916 had not imagined the talking pictures—or indeed the radio. The talking pictures—or picture plays—could be mechanically presented several times a day, seven days of the week. The theatre, governed by human limitations (and the Lord's Day Observance Act), could give, as a rule, only eight performances a week—and none on Sundays. Its prices had to be higher, but the higher the price the higher the tax—and the stronger the attraction of the talking picture.

In 1934 (11 June) Mr Chamberlain threw a hint of things

[1] Rate (1931): 1*s*. + 2½*d*.; 6*s*. + 1*s*. 3*d*.; 10*s*. 6*d*. + 2*s*. 2*d*.; 12*s*. 6*d*. + 2*s*. 6*d*.

to come: 'For my part', he said, 'I shall be glad, if my resources permit me to do so . . . to remodel the whole tax, because I think that in its present form it is unsatisfactory, both theoretically and practically.'

In 1935 he said: 'In these days, when the theatre has fallen on hard times in competition with a new form of entertainment, I certainly feel that one does not want to do anything to make the lot of the proprietor, producer, playwright or play actors any harder than it is. . . . I propose to relieve from all duty all payments up to 6*d*. . . . costing £2,300,000 in a full year. The remaining £400,000 I propose to apply entirely to the reduction of the duty on seats over 6*d*. in entertainments given by living performers. They have *claimed total exemption*; I cannot give them that, but I am sure they will not fail to appreciate the importance of a change which, for the first time, differentiates between this kind of performance and another, and differentiates in their favour.'[1]

They did not.

There seems to have been no opposition. Mr Attlee, replying, said, 'I was also pleased to see the change proposed in the entertainments duty, both in its effects on those occupying cheaper seats, and also, particularly, because of the remodelling of the tax in order to meet the case of living performers.'

Mr Holdsworth moved an amendment to extend the reduction in tax for seats over 6*d*. to 'a football or cricket match or other athletic or sporting contest or exhibition'. So there is nothing novel in the Labour Party's present policy, to put sport on the same level as the theatre. The amendment was defeated by 207 to 64.

(In this account, where, for brevity's sake, I use the expression 'the living theatre' the following official definition must be understood:

[1] Rate (1935): 1*s*. + 1½*d*.; 6*s*. + 1*s*. 2*d*.; 10*s*. 6*d*. + 2*s*.; 12*s*. 6*d*. + 2*s*. 5*d*. But note that in 1916 Mr McKenna put 1*s*. only on a 12*s*. 6*d*. ticket.

'Where all the performers whose words or actions constitute the entertainment are actually present and performing, and the entertainment consists solely of one or more of the following items, namely: (*a*) a stage play, (*b*) a ballet (whether a stage play or not), (*c*) a performance of music, (*d*) an Eisteddfod, (*e*) a lecture, (*f*) a recitation, (*g*) a music-hall or other variety entertainment, (*h*) a puppet or marionette show, (*i*) a circus, a travelling show, or menagerie.')

This distinction is a high peak in the story, and Mr Chamberlain deserves high honour from the theatre.

RATES OF DUTY—RISE AND FALL

In all there have been 13 different rates for the theatre. It may be convenient to leap ahead and display them together now. This table shows the rise and fall in the amounts of duty added to the theatre charge for seats (i.e. for payments exclusive of duty as defined in the Finance Acts) so that the charge payable for admission is the 'Original Charge' as shown plus the amount of duty. Up to 30 June 1935 one rate applied to all forms of entertainment but from 1 July 1935 an 'alternative rate' applied to the 'living theatre' and those rates are, therefore, shown from that date. The peak years were 1943-8.

Expressed in this way, as a kind of purchase, or rather sales tax, on the original price of the ticket, the duty has ranged from about 9 per cent in 1916 to 40-42 per cent in 1943-8, and 18 per cent today. Sir Kingsley Wood's proposed purchase tax on 'newspapers, periodicals and books' was to be at the rate of 16⅔ per cent.

Expressed as a percentage of the gross takings, the tax has ranged from 7-8 per cent in 1916 to 29-30 per cent in 1943-8 and 14-15 per cent today.

For comparative rates on the theatre, cinema, and sport in 1916, 1936, and 1956, see Appendix 'B'.

Duty operative as from:	*Original Charge* 1*s.*		2*s.* 6*d.*		5*s.*		6*s.*		10*s.* 6*d.*		12*s.* 6*d.*	
	s.	*d.*	*s.*	*d.*	*s.*	*d.*	*s.*	*d.*	*s.*	*d.*	*s.*	*d.*
1916 15th May		2		2		3		6	1	0	1	0
1917 1st Oct.		3		6		9	1	0	1	6	2	0
1918 1st Aug.		3		6		9	1	0	1	6	2	0
1919 1st Oct.		3		6		9	1	0	1	6	2	0
1924 24th June		2		6		9	1	0	1	6	2	0
1931 9th Nov.		2½		6	1	0	1	3	2	2	2	6
1935 1st July		1½		5		11	1	2	2	0	2	5
1939 3rd Sep.		½		4		10	1	0	1	11	2	4
1940 6th Oct.		1		5		11	1	2	2	0	2	5
1942 17th May		2		10	1	8	2	0	3	6	4	2
1943 16th May		2½		11	2	2	2	7	4	3	5	1
1948 30th May		Nil		4		10	1	0	1	11	2	4
1954 30th May		Nil		3½		9½		11½	1	10½	2	3½

1937

SIR JOHN SIMON

This humble person entered the House at the end of 1935. In my Election Address I had attacked the tax in general and declared for the abolition of the tax on the living theatre and music: and through all my time in Parliament (except for the war period) I did my best to honour my 'election pledges'. Each year, till the war came, a small but enthusiastic band of Members, drawn from all parties, attacked the tax in Committee on the Finance Bill. Mr (now Sir) William Mabane conducted the strategy, led the deputations, and discouraged me from unwise Divisions; and I made most of the indignant speeches. I should add that throughout this period we had the invaluable advice of Walter Payne, the President of the Society of West End Managers. There were also Mr Alexander, Mr Liddall, Mr Coleman, Mr Alfred Denville, and others. Sir William says he is not sure about this, but I would swear to it: late one night, when the debate, as usual, had gone all our way and he had been prowling round the building 'counting heads' he came to me and said: "For God's sake withdraw your motion! You'll defeat the Government!" (That, I think, was in 1938). Certainly, we made some headway, and always we had strong support from the Labour Opposition. Sir John Simon, the new Chancellor, who was a much better and greater man than most people ever knew, had a genuine affection for the theatre (and other arts), and, I am sure, disliked this tax. But for the war, I believe he would have abolished it.

In 1937 I tried a new technique. In Committee Mr Alfred Denville had moved a new Clause to abolish the tax (*Hansard*, Vol. 326, col. 437, 7 July 1937). He told the House that a memorial to the same effect had been signed by 300 Members—out of 615—and passed to the Chancellor. (In 1956 358 Members, more than half the House, went further, and put their names to a Motion on the Order Paper.) But to the Treasury the wishes of the three hundred Members were no more important than the buzzing of three hundred bees. The Minister said that the amendment would cost £1,250,000 in a full year: that 'this year is one of great financial strain, and although we listen sympathetically to this proposal we cannot accept it'. Mr Herbert Morrison said, 'A Division will be a test as to whether the 300 memorialists will back up the memorial or not.' Alas, when the Finance Bill—and the Whips—are on, memorials, and private opinions, have to be forgotten. The usual procedure followed. Mr Denville, a Government supporter, asked leave to withdraw his Clause. The Opposition said 'No', and in the Lobbies it was defeated by 192-130. Mr Denville did not vote.

Later, on the Report (another kind of Committee) stage I moved a new Clause, which I print in full, in case it may be of service to some future fighter:

'NEW CLAUSE (Entertainments Duty to terminate at end of the financial year).

Section one of the Finance (New Duties) Act 1916, and

section one of the Finance Act 1935 (which relate to Entertainments Duty) shall cease to have effect on the thirty-first day of March, nineteen hundred and thirty-eight. (Mr A. Herbert)'. (*Hansard*, Vol. 326, col. 1335, 14 July 1937)

(It would have been better, I see now, for practical reasons, to make the date 1 August 1938.)

This Clause caught the fancy of many. One merit of it was that it gave a legitimate opportunity for a second debate on the same subject. Another was that no one could say we were interfering with the sacred Budget, or adding to the 'financial strain' by reducing the revenue that year. We were simply compelling the Treasury to take thought. 'The idea is', I said, 'that the Chancellor of the Exchequer, when preparing his new Budget, would be forced to say to himself, "At last, 21 years after this temporary tax was first imposed, it has, by the will of Parliament, been permitted to lapse, and now what am I to do—am I to impose it again in its present form or in some better form, or am I to impose half of it, or to impose it on some entertainments and not on others: or is there some new and delightful alternative source of revenue?" '

You can imagine what pain it gives me to quote my own speeches: but I then made some shy remarks in support of Mr Chamberlain's estimate of the tax, some of which, I feel, may be useful to other orators during the next fifty years:

'First of all, it is a bad tax in principle and in essence. It is not a tax which protects home industries; it is not a tax which keeps out the foreigner; it is not even a tax which, like the whisky tax or the tobacco tax, discourages certain indulgences which certain people regarded as vicious and harmful. Whatever we may say about this entertainment or that, this tax is a tax upon things of the mind. It is a tax upon the free communication of thought, ideas and knowledge, and to a very large extent and in a very true sense, it is a tax upon education. It is very difficult indeed to distinguish this tax from the old Taxes on Knowledge, as they were called, which we abolished, after a protracted and bitter struggle, only as long ago as the 1850's and the 1860's. It was in about 1850 that there ceased to be a tax upon every newspaper and every pamphlet that published news, and a tax upon advertisements, the chief source of revenue of newspapers, and upon paper, their raw material. Those taxes were rightly called Taxes upon Knowledge.

'It is safe to say that if anybody proposed to reimpose a tax of that sort at this stage, for instance, a tax upon books, say 20 per cent on the retail price of a 7*s*. 6*d*. novel, making a total price of 9*s*.—unless it was a novel by my humble self, about which nobody would bother—I think that tax would be regarded as monstrous and barbarous.[1] Yet it is difficult to find any argument for placing taxes upon concerts, music, drama and art and not placing them on books and newspapers; for, much as I admire newspapers, to which I contribute from time to time a diffident word or two, it is very difficult to say that all of them are solely educational. The great *Times* itself becomes more and more an entertainment, but it would be resented very bitterly if one had to pay a halfpenny tax on a twopenny *Times*.

'This is a bad tax because in selecting entertainments it makes no allowance whatever for the element of mind or culture, or whatever one may like to call it. If a man presents *Hamlet* or *A Midsummer Night's Dream* by the poet Shakespeare—an extremely risky thing to do—it is entertainment. If a man catches a couple of live monkeys, and exhibits them to the public in a cage, that is entertainment. If a man organises a great orchestra which plays the music of Bach, Beethoven and Mozart, that again is entertainment. If his flat windows command a view of the Boat Race or a State funeral or procession, that is, or at least used to be, entertainment. I well remember one occasion when, at a State funeral, entertainments tax was charged on those who let out rooms from which people could behold that spectacle. If a man gives the first performance of a new

[1] I failed, I confess, to foresee Sir Kingsley Wood (see page 41).

British symphony or opera that, again, is entertainment. If he races dogs, or keeps live lions, that is entertainment. I am not saying that some of these exhibitions are not properly taxed. What I am saying is that in a country which was really civilized it would be impossible to justify that kind of classification, which ignores any kind of element of mind or instructive quality.

'I ask hon. Members to consider how illogical is the tax. Consider the very terms of the Statute which originally imposed it. I cannot too often repeat that this tax was originally imposed under the special stress of the Great War. It was hastily devised, and it has been suffered patiently by those concerned, because of the circumstances of its introduction during the Great War. But in that Statute it was recognised that a great part of entertainment might be educational, because it was laid down that where an entertainment is wholly educational in character or is not conducted for profit, no tax is chargeable. No tax is charged on a production of a play by the poet Shakespeare at the "Old Vic". That goes free, and I am delighted that it should be so, but if the same play were produced in the West End then, suddenly, for some obscure reason, in the eyes of the authorities it ceases to be educational, because an attempt is being made to secure a profit on the performance. But the illogicality of the whole thing proceeds to extremes when you find that even if a wretched man makes a loss on presenting a play of Shakespeare's, he still has to pay the tax. I use the term "educational" seriously, because education is not merely a matter of going to school and studying school books. . . .

'I could give many illustrations of the various illogical results of this piece of legislation. I mention only one which is not very important, but which is good as an illustration. The House may know that all over the country there are social or literary societies which engage odd persons like myself to deliver instructive lectures. As long as the society is not conducted for profit and the lecture is considered to be generally educational, no tax is charged. In my younger days I used to deliver a lecture which was entitled, unfortunately, "On Being Funny". There was nothing very funny about it. I have never pretended to be a funny man. I am just like the rest of us—an ordinary nice chap who seeks to do good—and this lecture was of a rather high-brow character. It set out to explain the Bergsonian theory of laughter and the essence of humour and all that kind of thing, and I can say that the laughs which that lecture excited, even on the North-East Coast, were very rare indeed. But the vigilant officer of Customs and Excise, part of whose duties it is to look after these matters on the North-East Coast, pricked up his ears when he heard of this lecture entitled "On Being Funny". He said to himself: "There is something extremely deleterious and dangerous here." So he sent a report of this event to the Custom House in Billingsgate where, I understand, there is a special department which inspects, and, if necessary, disinfects the lectures to be delivered by literary men on the North-East Coast and other places. According to common form I was requested to supply a précis of my lecture in order to assure the Custom House, first, that it was educational and, secondly, that it was not at all amusing. To my astonishment, knowing how little entertainment that lecture appeared to afford to the public, I was unable to convince them of the second part of the proposition. The unhappy society had to pay tax upon the lecture, and I was never invited to lecture there again. That illustrates the strange idea that anything which is at all entertaining is something in the nature of an offence on which a fine ought to be imposed.

'So much for the principle of the tax. Another objection to it is on the ground of its incidence. I must remind hon. Members that this tax is levied not upon profits but upon receipts. Listening to recent discussions on the National Defence Contribution which, whatever its defects, is a tax upon profits, I have wondered how the representatives of business and industry would like a tax of 20 per cent, not on what goes into the savings bank but on what comes into the till. How would they like a tax which is not even levied upon receipts while profits are being gained, but is also levied upon those receipts even where a loss is being made?

'It may be said that the tax is paid by the consumer, but, in general, that is not so. Here, again, I have the authority of the late Chancellor of the Exchequer, though I cannot give the reference. . . .

'I want to say that the objections to this tax are not based on material grounds only. It is not only a question of damaging enterprise and employment, although, Heaven knows, those are important considerations. There is another form of damage as well. Here, I think, is a case in which the House of Commons can do something to improve the quality of dramatic and artistic entertainment whether in plays, in cinemas, in concerts, or in whatever form it may be. It is easy to find fault with any particular entertainment. You may say, Sir, that, judging by the last show you have seen, some particular entertainments ought to be taxed more severely, in fact taxed out of existence. Unfortunately that is not how things work. This kind of burden bears most heavily upon the better kind of entertainment. The greater the burden the greater the risk in these very speculative enterprises, and the greater the risk the greater the temptation to produce what is crude and vulgar, and, as those responsible may think, more likely to captivate the public mind. . . .'

Sir John Simon replied himself, courteous, kind, and even flattering. 'The hon. Member', he said, 'spoke of this as a bad tax. But does he know of a good tax? Is there a good tax? All taxes, in my view, are evil. . . . My hon. Friend made an important point when he urged that this tax has an unthinking and automatic operation. . . . I agree that it is a misfortune that you should have an instrument of taxation which hits—I will not say the just and the unjust—

but the finest and most beautiful examples of art and culture in exactly the same way as it hits very much more vulgar, less elaborate or less well contrived forms of entertainment. But how are you going to do otherwise? . . . I hope that it may be possible to dispense with certain taxes next year. But we cannot very well in advance declare that this is the one instrument in the whole collection of instruments of torture which we will here and now abolish. I am sorry not to be more obliging . . . and no one is more sorry to oppose his brilliant ideas. . . . But . . .' The Committee divided: Ayes, 118: Noes, 207.

1938

The following year, 1938, I put down the same new Clause, but this time in Committee (Vol. 337, col. 2237). I filled nine columns of *Hansard*, and Mr Mabane ably seconded the Clause, which was strongly supported by Members of all parties. Mr Ralph Assheton, I see, said 'A tax on plays is as uncivilized as a tax on books'.

Sir John Simon was still more sympathetic. 'I do share a great deal of the feeling against this particular form of tax. . . . I will offer the assurance that I will during the year have the working of these taxes studied from every point of view, recognizing, as I do, that there is great force in this argument, especially as applied to the living theatre. . . .' And his last words were, 'I share the feeling that, really and truly in this country, this ancient home of culture, art and literature, this tax ought not to be allowed automatically to continue without very serious examination.'

We had, we felt, made a real impression this time. Once more, nudged by Mabane, I 'begged leave to withdraw' the Clause. Once more, the Opposition cried 'No!' We did better in this Division: Ayes, 115: Noes, 191.

1939

Sir John Simon was as good as his word, and in his 1939 Budget he did give another slight relief:[1]

'The chief difficulty under which the living theatre labours is the rival attraction of the cinema. At the same time I realize that the Duty does aggravate the disability from which the living theatre suffers, and Parliament, I think, would wish, if it could, to help.'[2]

'He has given us', I said, 'one-quarter of what we asked for. The total abolition of the tax would mean a loss of revenue of £1,250,000, and he is losing £300,000 in a full year.' But we were rearming madly. 'It would have been a fine thing, as we said when we went to him on a deputation, if at this grave time, when we are compelled to spend these incredible and unprecedented sums on weapons of destruction, he had been able to say, "We are not pressed so far by that barbarous necessity that we cannot afford to take away altogether what is generally regarded as an undesirable tax upon the things of the mind".'

That, after all, was what we said later, when his successor sought to tax newspapers and books. But, at that grim time, it was a handsome gesture (of which, I am sure, the Treasury did not approve), and I thanked Sir John warmly. The theatre should remember Sir John Simon very kindly.

That, I see, was the famous day of 'The Monkey and the Bishop'. Whenever doubters, or opponents, said: 'But how are we going to raise the revenue we lose?' (an illegitimate question, by the way), I answered, 'By a betting tax'. I went on about that now. I finished—or nearly finished—pretty strongly:

'What is going to happen if war comes? Is this vast

[1] Rate (1939): 1*s*. + ½*d*.; 6*s*. + 1*s*.; 10*s*. 6*d*. + 1*s*. 11*d*.; 12*s*.6*d*. + 2*s*. 4*d*.

[2] Vol. 346, col. 991, 25 April 1939.

business of betting to go on uncontrolled and untaxed while every other activity is rendering its appropriate due to the revenue? I do not know. I conclude by congratulating the Chancellor of the Exchequer on the Budget, which, I think, on the whole, will have a very fine reception, and I thank him in particular for what he has done for the living theatre: but it still remains true that all the productive earnings and industry of the people are taxed, that music and the drama are taxed not only on their profits but on their losses; while this, to say the least, improvident activity, rising to the enormous height of £400,000,000 a year, goes absolutely free. God forbid that I should have a Government job; but if the Government will make me their unofficial agent, and give me Government time to push a Measure through, I will square the bookmakers and the bishops—one are my friends and the others are my constituents. If I am given a free hand by His Majesty's Government I will undertake to get that Bill through and make it a foundation upon which in a normal year they can get £20,000,000 of revenue. . . .'

I then found myself in a familiar but alarming situation—I did not know what my last words were to be. I may have prepared some powerful peroration: but, if so, it escaped me then. To my astonishment, I heard myself saying:

'And, as the monkey said to the Bishop, "I can't say fairer than that." '

The House laughed uproariously and long. Many Members, and very many correspondents, begged me to tell them just why the monkey had made that remark to the Bishop. I had to tell them that I had not the faintest idea.

The House laughed also, no doubt, at my boastful undertaking. But last year (1955) the tax on certain corners of betting—on football pools, dog-racing totalisators and bookmakers—a partial, illogical and unjust tax—yielded nearly £29,000,000. 'So' as they say, 'there!' Today, if the thing were done properly, my figure would be more like £60,000,000. The total yield of Entertainments Duty—on everything—is only £41,000,000. 'But,' you may say, "is not a tax on betting another "Fine on Fun"?' Yes, dear reader, and so are the taxes on smoking and 'drinking'. When I am dictator of my own Utopia these indulgences also may be free: but, meanwhile, I must distinguish between such material or fleshly pleasures and the spiritual or harmless joys like listening to music and watching plays or games. I predict that, one day, Whitehall will act accordingly. And, as the monkey said to the Bishop, . . . etc.

But, undeterred by this concession, or the talk of war, Mr George Hall (Labour) proposed to abolish the tax on the living theatre. (Note the date, 22 June 1939.)

'I think the Chancellor', he said, 'should go the whole hog and repeal the duty altogether. . . . I can enjoy a film almost as well as a play but sometimes one wants to see the real thing.'

Mr Benson (Labour) usefully compared the incidence of the tax in theatre and cinema:[1]

'In spite of the Chancellor's concession the incidence of taxation upon the living theatre is very much higher than it is on the cinema.

'If hon. Members will compare the two Schedules, their first impression will be that the living theatre pays a less proportion of its receipts in taxation than does the cinema, but in actual fact that is not so. The living theatre pays a very much higher proportion of its receipts in taxation, notwithstanding the different Schedules, than does the cinema, and for this reason. The cinema has a continuous performance. The performance may start in the morning, as it does in the Tatler theatres and in some of the ordinary cinema theatres in London, and run on until nearly midnight. They have a 10 or 12-hour day, and there is a continuous

[1] Vol. 348, col. 2551.

influx and outflow of patrons. A 6*d.* seat in one of these cinemas on which there is no taxation may be occupied four, five, six, or even more, times a day . . . The 6*d.* seat in the cinema may produce a revenue of 3*s.*, 4*s.*, or 5*s.* a day and it pays no taxation, but a similar revenue from a seat in the living theatre will be subjected to a charge of 10*d.* or 1*s.* in taxation. Right throughout the whole scale the prices of seats in the living theatre have to be high because of the single performance as against the continuous performance and the larger number of shows run per day in the cinema.'

Mr Silverman, and the indefatigable Alfred Denville, supported them, but Captain Crookshank, Financial Secretary, thought that the whole affair was rather ungrateful.

Ayes, 138: Noes, 201.

III

The (Second) War

1940

SIR KINGSLEY WOOD

THEN the war came, and on 23 July 1940 Sir John's successor, Sir Kingsley Wood, among other bigger and better taxes, put another £4,000,000 on the Entertainments Duty generally,[1] of which £250,000 was to come from 'Living Entertainments'.[2] The principle of a differential rate for the living theatre was retained: and I am glad to record that Sir Kingsley did not sound the same Puritanical note as the legislators of 1916:

'I should like to say to the Committee and to the country that the increase in Entertainments Duty is not designed to discourage persons from having and enjoying the entertainments available to them. It is rather a contribution which I believe they will willingly make towards those defences which make it possible to enjoy, with their families and friends, reasonable relaxation and pleasure.'

Later, on the Finance (No. 2) Bill, Mr Alfred Denville still spluttered valiantly (Vol. 364, col. 470—8 August 1940). He spoke of '400 signatories' who had been ignored. 'It is rather disconcerting and lowers one's pride when one

[1] Vol. 363, col. 648.

[2] Rate (1940): 1*s.* + 1*d.*; 6*s.* + 1*s.* 2*d.*; 10*s.* 6*d.* + 2*s.* 0*d.*; 12*s.* 6*d.* + 2*s.* 5*d.* (on living theatre).

feels that a large body of Members of this House are treated like children and are not consulted at all. . . .'

But the theatrical world, as always in time of war, loyally took its poison, and, according to Sir Kingsley 'raised no objection at present in view of national needs'.

In reply to Mr Denville, he said—a pleasing passage: 'No Chancellor of the Exchequer could say that certain taxes would be remitted after the war. Equally no Chancellor of the Exchequer could say . . . that they are to remain on for all time. I hope conditions may be such that in due course we may be able to mitigate taxes of this kind, because it is a matter of regret that the theatre particularly should be affected in this way.'

Mr Pethick-Lawrence, for the Labour Party, said: 'The Committee is accepting this proposal in view of the national need, but I am sure the Chancellor of the Exchequer will not take it that, because there is no opposition in the form of a vote, that gives him an indefinite right on future occasions to go on putting up the tax during the war.'

But it did.

NEWSPAPERS AND BOOKS

In 1940, too, poor Sir Kingsley Wood, most ill-advised by his Treasury men, made another proposal which is highly relevant to our purpose; and here is, besides, a golden episode in the history of the British Parliament.

On 23 July 1940 (Vol. 363, col. 652) the Chancellor announced that he proposed to introduce 'two rates' of Purchase Tax 'sharply differential'. There would be a 'high rate of tax'—$33\frac{1}{3}$ per cent—on luxuries . . . like furs, lace, fancy goods, jewellery, etc., and a half-rate ($16\frac{2}{3}$ per cent on the wholesale value) on articles like boots and shoes (other than children's).

'Domestic hollow-ware like pots, pans and kettles will be taxed at only half rate, as also will cups, saucers and plates, if made of earthenware; if made of china or porcelain they will be charged at the full rate. Domestic brooms and brushes will be charged at the reduced rate of duty. In addition I propose to include at the lower rate medicines and drugs other than those completely exempt: and finally newspapers, periodicals and books. This places at the lower rate those personal and household goods which require fairly frequent replacements.'

So 'newspapers, periodicals, and books' were introduced at the end of a list which began with 'domestic hollow-ware'. I have a feeling that the insult was intentional: for in this affair the cherubic, genial Sir Kingsley was testy and, for a time, defiant. On July 2 (Vol. 362, col. 676), Mr Lindsay (Combined English Universities) had asked him 'whether he will exclude books from the scope of the forthcoming Purchase Tax, in view of the absolute dependence of book exports on the volume of home trade, and the vital importance of this industry, both at home and overseas, to the morale of the English-speaking peoples?"

Sir Kingsley Wood: 'I have given careful and sympathetic consideration to the matter, but I regret that I cannot exempt the publishing trade from making this contribution to the revenue needed for the prosecution of the war.'

Mr. Lindsay: 'Without putting the matter out of perspective, will my right hon. Friend reconsider his answer, in view of the fact that this is, in a very real sense, a tax on knowledge?'

Then there was a deputation of important (and 'disinterested') persons, led by the Archbishop of Canterbury. But even then Sir Kingsley Wood, it seems, saw nothing in this affair but the selfish complaints of 'the publishing trade'. I am told that, as the deputation left, the Archbishop turned and said 'You've not heard the end of this, Mr Chancellor, not by a long chalk.'

The storm grew. On the Budget Resolutions Sir Percy

Harris (that good old Liberal) said (Vol. 363, col. 672): 'I regret that he has not thrown over the tax on what is not a luxury but a necessity in war-time, the tax on books . . . this very bad tax on knowledge. . . .' Mr Lipson (Ind.) said (col. 692):

'I would like to ask him whether he is imposing this tax on books and newspapers because he wants to restrict consumption. Does he want people to read less? The amount involved cannot be very great, but the principle involved is a vital one. This is an old battle that has been fought out before, for it really is a tax on knowledge at a time when there should be no such tax.'

Sir Stanley Reed (*Aylesbury*): 'Does my hon. Friend ask the Committee to believe that one-tenth of the matter published as books today is any contribution whatever to knowledge?'

Mr Lipson: 'That is not the point, because it is proposed to tax the good with the bad . . .'

But Conservatives were not very helpful and on July 25 Sir George Broadbridge (City of London) said (col. 1025):

'With regard to books and all the fuss that has been made about the suggested tax, I can see nothing to which to take exception. Generally speaking, reading is a hobby. Most of the business in books, in any event, is done with libraries. Apart from books and reading, I have a hobby, which is either golf or tennis. Every time I play I have to pay a substantial sum for the pleasure of doing it. If I have to pay for my hobby, surely book readers can pay something for theirs.'

I had got a day's leave from my little ship at Holehaven, and now, I see, fired off a few observations (col. 1040):

'I approach the subject with some sense of delicacy, as one who was, at least, a professional author, but I approach it with a good conscience, because since the war began I have not been able to write books, and as long as His Majesty requires my services elsewhere it is not likely that I shall be able to write one. Also, as a representative of that great centre of light and learning, Oxford University, I feel that I may say something on this matter.

'I hope that the relations of Oxford and the City of London will always continue to be friendly, but when I hear the representative of the City of London referring to a tax on books, the "machine-tools of education", as someone has said, of the great craft of literature, the great profession of learning, as a tax upon a mere "hobby", to be compared with golf, then that is a mind with which I can make no contact, and I do not propose to try. I address myself, with much more confidence, to the Chancellor of the Exchequer. Great qualities, such as geniality and tact, have carried the right hon. Gentleman from one office to another, with the good will of all and the hopes of many, as you may see some cheery reveller staggering from "pub" to "pub", emerging from each with such a radiant smile that no one has the heart to stop his passage to the next. But, in this affair, without intention, I am sure, he has added insult to injury.

'After receiving a deputation of the highest authority, led by the Archbishop of Canterbury and including men of the greatest light and learning, he dismissed the whole thing as if it were merely a question of "the publishing trade" having to suffer the same as other trades. There is much more in it than that. . . .

'. . . I have been sent a copy of *The Bookseller*, on the front page of which is written:

' "*Books are part of the cause for which we fight*—Dear Mr Segrave, I am very glad to know that the list of books to be published here during the summer and autumn is, as usual, going out this year to carry the reminder that freedom to write and read is part of the cause for which the British Empire and Commonwealth fights. . . . Duff Cooper."[1]

[1] Then Minister of Information.

'Which is the right horse here? I am anxious to find out what is in those woolly heads. Does the right hon. Gentleman desire, or does he not desire, in his extraordinary language, to limit the civilian consumption of domestic hollow-ware, brushes, brooms, and, as he said finally, with that charming smile, books. Does he really desire to "limit the consumption" of Bibles and Prayer Books? I suppose I cannot get an answer to that? If he does, there is still a niche in that Lobby, and he may go down in history as the first Chancellor of the Exchequer to put a tax on the Word of God. . . .'

(Some members thought that this was fanciful and unfair, but later, on 30 July, Commander King-Hall asked the Chancellor 'whether it is intended that the Bible will be subject to the Purchase Tax?'

Sir K. Wood: 'Yes, Sir. Income Tax is payable on the profits of the sales of Bibles by commercial publishers and booksellers, and the liability of such books to the Purchase Tax would seem no less equitable as a contribution to the war effort.')

I repeat some more of my remarks, without shame, for there is hardly a word which is not equally applicable to the theatre tax (Vol. 363, col. 1042):

'The Chancellor himself, and the Minister of Information are desirous that the export trade should continue; and the export trade is surprisingly large—about half the home trade. Now, may I observe, for the hundredth time, that a book is not like a bottle of whisky; nor indeed, is it much like domestic hollow-ware. You might well say, "We shall not sell any whisky in England; we shall keep it all for export and send it to the United States." That, I imagine, could be done effectively; but you cannot do that with books, because the export of books depends on a prosperous home industry. No one would publish a book of mine purely for publication in America. The export trade is a kind of overflow from the main basin. So, if you seriously damage the home trade in books, you may say goodbye to your export trade. . . .

'My hon. Friend says that the result of the tax will be fewer bad books and more good books. The contrary will be the result. It is the "trashy modern novel", or at least the sensational success, which carries the losses on the portentous and no doubt more worthy works. . . . Two book publishers have gone out of business, and one was the publisher of the great War Memoirs of the right hon. Gentleman the Member for Carnarvon Boroughs (Mr Lloyd George). It is a pity that they did not have a few trashy novels to keep them in business. . . . I am not going to say that all publishers in London will go out of business, though two have gone and there certainly will be more, but there will be fewer books, and fewer good books. I say further, that if but one good book, one good writer, one new thought and one new invention is held back from the public by this tax, it is bad and barbarous and ought to be abolished. I am not thinking so much of pennies as of principles.

'I was reminding the right hon. Gentleman just now of a book that I have here, *The History of the Taxes on Knowledge*, with which I hope the Treasury officials will try to become acquainted, because they seem to have forgotten, if they ever knew, that it is only 70 or 80 years since the great fight against the taxes on knowledge was fought and won in this House. . . .

'It is a sad and shocking thing that at this time in this titanic conflict, when we are saying, and saying truly, that there are arrayed, on one side, the spirit of force and, on the other, the forces of the Spirit, we should have sunk so low as to be seeking to treat all learning and enlightened literature in the same way as we should treat brooms or something which is kept under the bed. The right hon. Gentleman had a great opportunity. He might have said,

"However many Hitlers are at the door, however many dangers and difficulties confront us, we are not so down and out and so poor in resources that for the sake of £500,000—which is my estimate of the yield of this miserable tax—we are going to do this barbarous thing."

'Well may the shades of Milton, of Caxton, of Sheridan and of Charles Dickens, and of those brave men, who in the last century fought and won the principle of free enlightenment, groan in their honoured graves today to think that that lamp which they hung on the walls of Westminster has been clumsily torn down at last by a Chancellor of the Exchequer who, at this hour of civilization, sees no important distinction between boots and books.'

'Sound and fury' said the Chancellor later; but it was needed. Viscount Wolmer (Con.) rebuked me very severely (col. 1048):

'The consumption of books must be curtailed just as much as the consumption of other things which are necessary to human life as we understand it—and I certainly put books in that category. The Chancellor of the Exchequer must assist in the curtailing process by this tax on the purchase of all commodities.'

My estimate of the revenue was erroneous. On 1 August (col. 1413) Sir Kingsley told me that:

'The revenue estimated to accrue in a full year from the application of the Purchase Tax to newspapers, periodicals and books is approximately as follows: Newspapers (including Sunday and weekly newspapers), and periodicals, between £3,250,000 and £3,500,000. Books, between £1,000,000 and £1,250,000.'

Sir E. Graham-Little asked the Chancellor of the Exchequer whether, 'if he cannot exempt books altogether from the proposed Purchase Tax, he will at least exclude from its operation medical, scientific and school books necessary for professional and educational purposes?'

Sir K. Wood: 'I am afraid any discrimination between different classes of books would be impracticable.' (col. 1414)

(But the Chancellor's minions of Customs and Excise were still, at that date, 'discriminating between different classes of plays', and when it is a question of 'wholly educational' still are.)

Sir Kingsley was stung by these assaults but still unshaken. The story was at that time that the Chancellor, maddened by Archbishops, University Members, and incomprehensible talk about 'Taxes on Knowledge', intended to stick his toes in. 'I shall tell them in Committee, if they're not careful, they're lucky I'm not taxing books at the higher rate.'

But on 13 August—note, by the way, the date: while the Commons bravely fought the Treasury, Hitler was at Boulogne, the Battle of Britain was imminent, and down at Canvey Island the little Water Gipsy, with her one machine-gun, two rifles, and two cutlasses, was part of a 'striking force' against invasion—the Chancellor surrendered.

Mr Isaacs (Southwark, North), a printer (afterwards Minister of Labour), moved to leave out lines 38 to 53, and made a good speech which he cut short, because Sir Kingsley had already dropped a hint (Vol. 364, col. 746):

'The printing industry', said Mr Isaacs, 'has been described as the "art preservative of all arts." . . . We want all literature free of tax. . . . I ask that newspapers shall not be taxed. . . . The main question is that of retaining a free Press.'

Sir Kingsley had seen the red light and rose at once (Vol. 364, col. 747). He was a little grudging and for once seemed wounded:

'I must say that I feel a good deal of the sound and fury has been unjustifiable.'

He would have nothing to do with the 'principle' on

which, in fact, he had been compelled to yield. '*I cannot accept the contention that the printed word should necessarily be immune from taxation. . . .*' I was back at Canvey Island, but I read with pleasure his shrewd thrust at my peroration:

'. . . If the time comes when we have to choose between money for books, and money for such despised articles as boots, or between magazines and milk, then we shall have to choose boots and milk, and, with all due respect to some of my hon. Friends, that choice will be right.'

He stuck to the 'objective reasons' and 'the economic case' and swallowed them whole, including much of my own 'sound and fury'—for example, on the 'export trade' in books: "For a book to be a successful export, it must also provide a lucrative investment at home' (col. 750). And he concluded:

'Finally, I do not under-estimate the importance to be attached to the publication of valuable but unremunerative books, which is only justified and made possible by the sale of less original, but more fashionable works.' (My 'trashy novels'!) 'I can appreciate arguments of this kind, and, while there is much to be said to the contrary, in view of the considerations to which I have referred, which do not apply to other articles in the Schedule, I think that, on the whole, I should agree that books, as well as newspapers, should be exempt from the tax—at least, for the present.'

'At least for the present'—a sinister note, which newspapers should remember—especially those who think that the Entertainments Tax is good and proper. One day some panic-stricken Chancellor may say: 'If I can tax the play, why not the Press?'

Two points of great power emerge from this long story:

(1) Whenever Parliament (that is, the 'private' or unofficial Members of all parties) chooses to assert itself, it can defeat Whitehall and the Whips on a financial

matter—even with the enemy at the gates: and the pity is that the sovereign Parliament does not say 'Boo!' to the Treasury more often.

(2) However little Sir Kingsley Wood liked it, however smoothly he shrugged it off, it was the intellectual, not the material, case that defeated him—the 'Tax on Thought', not the 'Injury to Trade'.

If there were really no difference between 'the publishing trade' and 'the domestic hollow-ware trade', he could have 'charged on regardless'. But, one way and another, the difference was drummed into that stubborn little mind. There is a lesson here for 'entertainment' folk of all sorts everywhere: 'Mix the bowling. Explain by all means that the tax is bankrupting—but rub it in as well that it is barbarous; for both are true.'

And, whenever anyone defends the Entertainment Tax, remember 1940, and say 'How about newspapers and books?'

In 1942[1] Sir Kingsley Wood said he proposed to double the Entertainments Duty. But this too simple formula was readjusted slightly for the general convenience, and accepted by Sir Irving Albery for the theatre 'as a purely wartime measure'.[2] [3]

In 1943, again, Sir Kingsley Wood said:[4] 'I am increasing Entertainments Duty both on the full scale applicable to cinemas, etc., and on the reduced scale applicable to theatres and other living entertainments.' But all seats up to 1*s.* were sacred.

The new rates were colossal—the highest peak:

[1] Vol. 379, cols. 136-7.

[2] Vol. 379, col. 1977, 14 May 1942.

[3] Rate (1942): 1*s.* + 2*d.*; 6*s.* + 2*s.*; 10*s.* 6*d.* + 3*s.* 6*d.*; 12*s.* 6*d.* + 4*s.* 2*d.*

[4] Vol. 388, col. 972.

I. LIVING THEATRE, CIRCUSES, ETC.

Amount of payment excluding amount of duty		*Rate of Duty*		*Full Payment*	
s.	*d.*	*s.*	*d.*	*s.*	*d.*
1	0		2½	1	2½
6	0	2	7	8	7
10	6	4	3	14	9
12	6	5	1	17	7

II. CINEMA AND SPORT

Amount of payment excluding amount of duty		*Rate of Duty*		*Full Payment*	
s.	*d.*	*s.*	*d.*	*s.*	*d.*
3	2	2	7	5	9
5	0	4	7	9	7

These rates remained till 1948.

In Committee[1] Mr John Dugdale moved an amendment to put 'games' on the same level and 'rate' as the living theatre. The Financial Secretary (Mr Ralph Assheton) said: 'The object of giving a reduced rate of tax for the living stage was to help the living stage in competition with the cinema, and that still stands as the justification for it. . . . The reason is to protect the living stage.' Amendment rejected.

Mr Frankel[2] made, I think, the first attempt to get amateur sport classed with the theatre.

Mr Assheton said again:

'The grounds on which the original concession was made were the protection of the living theatre against the cinema. I do not think there is any reason to suppose that amateur football or cricket needs protection against the cinema. . . .' Amendment rejected.

Mr Clement Davies (Liberal) struck a new and original note:[3]

[1] Vol. 390, col. 229, 2 June 1943.

[2] Vol. 390, col. 236. [3] Vol. 390, col. 239-40.

'I wish to enter a protest which I have done before . . . against Entertainments Duty in wartime. At such a time Entertainments Duty is a bad tax. . . . One of the effects of a tax is to act as a deterrent. For example, the taxes on tobacco, beer and spirits should cut down consumption, and that is right because a good deal of labour and material is required. . . . But that cannot be so with regard to entertainments. Entertainment, instead of being deterred, should be encouraged, and the Government recognize that with regard to certain forms of entertainment, because all the time they are encouraging entertainment to the troops and inside the factories. Why not, therefore, encourage it throughout? They realise that entertainment is necessary to maintain morale, and I protest against the continuance of this tax in time of war. . . .'

Sir Kingsley Wood, however, testified once more[1] to the loyal alacrity with which theatre and cinema had accepted his proposals. 'They responded admirably. . . .' He concluded: 'I hope the country will continue to enjoy this form of relaxation, for there is no reason why we should live in a state of gloom during the war. . . ." Rather different speeches from 1916, but the same tax—only more of it. Mr McKenna (1916) charged 1*s.* on a 12*s.* 6*d.* ticket. Sir Kingsley was now charging 5*s.* 1*d.*

1943–1945

SIR JOHN ANDERSON

In the last years of the war Sir John Anderson, who succeeded Sir Kingsley Wood, had some administrative trouble with the tax, but this will be considered, more conveniently, under '1946—The Zoo-Clause'.

[1] Vol. 390, col. 243.

IV

After the (Second) War

1946

DR DALTON

IN 1946 Dr Dalton (Chancellor of the Exchequer), with the best will in the world, made two more 'mutilations'.

(1) *Shakespeare and Billiards*

Mr Chamberlain's 1935 concession to the 'living theatre' had been made upon 'cultural'—or, I suppose, 'partly educational'—grounds, to give it a fairer fight with the film. But the sports folk, logically enough, said 'We're "living" too': and now they were admitted into the Shakespeare class.

Dr Dalton, in his Budget speech (Vol. 421, col. 1825—9 April 1946) said: 'I propose that the lower scale shall now apply to football, cricket, boxing, tennis, swimming; in short to all outdoor sports—including the University Boat Race—except horse, motor and dog-racing. Horse, motor and dog-racing will continue, with the cinema, to pay at the higher rate. . . . I should add that the reduced scale will apply also to indoor games such as billiards and chess. This concession will cost £1,000,000 this year, and £1,250,000 in a full year. I believe that it is well worth the money, in the interests of British sport, recreation, and physical fitness.'

I do not think that many objected to this. But it was one more lapse of logic—or rather, several. Why relieve the man who watches Arsenal and not the man who watches the Derby? Is it more 'educational' to watch professional billiards than the Gold Cup at Ascot?

On these lines, I see that I made a few remarks (Vol. 424, col. 264), which, I think, may deserve a place in the dossier, for they record an important stage in the moral decline and fall of the Duty:

'I am not opposing the Clause, because it is a genial gesture from the Chancellor, and it would be unpleasant and impolitic to be ungrateful to such a gesture from that necessarily frosty quarter. In the original Act, the Finance Act of 1916, by which Entertainments Duty was first imposed as a temporary measure for the last war but one—and an undertaking was given by the Chancellor of that time that it would come to an end after the war—the only exemptions had relation to educational or, to use a word I do not like, "cultural", things. Those exemptions were mainly intended to protect such institutions as the Zoo, the learned and cultural associations, lecture societies, museums, and so on. In 1935 Parliament introduced an exceptional relief for the living theatre which was then, as it is now, and always will be, gravely menaced by films, especially American. All the exemptions were for mental entertainment, with the circus as perhaps a borderline case. . . .

'But let us see what a logical fog we are getting ourselves into. . . .

There seems to be no sense whatever in these distinctions. A profit-making commercial boxing contest is now to be classed with the intellectual theatre as a cultural entertainment and will pay the same rate as the theatre. I do not mind, but really we must realise what we are doing. Take the horse, the noble animal. The horse, if seen in the circus doing ignoble antics which I hate seeing it do, is taxed at 42 per cent[1] on a 5*s.* ticket; but if he is doing what he was

[1] 42 per cent, that is, on the price of the ticket without the duty: it was about 30 per cent of the price paid.

designed by God to do, running very fast over the grass ridden by a fine rider, the tax is 91 per cent. What is the sense in that distinction? Boxing, you may say, is a noble sport; I agree, but what about billiards, the moral effect of which upon the young has been a byword for decades? Billiards, the only game which is by law prohibited on licensed premises on Sundays, becomes an intellectual pastime to be taxed at the lower rate. . . .

'. . . All these things add up to the conclusion that there are so many anomalies that it is no good tinkering with this old kettle and it would be better to throw it away. I am not against cricket and football being relieved. I am not taking the intellectual line at all. . . . All these entertainments are not like businesses which sell hot water bottles, or thermos flasks, or something else for which there is a regular demand. They are enterprises subject to all sorts of hazards like the weather, Royal processions, and Heaven knows what besides. It is therefore wrong to lay such a heavy tax on turnover upon them with no regard to whether the business is making a profit or a loss.

'Finally, the reason why I think this Clause ought to be rejected is that it is against the whole purpose for which we are here. *What are we here for*? In the old phrase, "life, liberty and the pursuit of happiness". We talk about work for all, but we do not mean work for all; much as we admire and glorify work, we mean such work for all as will enable them to have happy leisure—happy evenings and happy Sundays, and every kind of mental and physical refreshment. . . . But whether the producers of these refreshments are making a profit or a loss, we put upon them this swingeing tax of 42 per cent. We are making this tax like a leaky old boat; the more you patch it the more it leaks and the uglier it looks, and from that point of view I am pleased with this new tinkering, because one day I think some wise Chancellor of the Exchequer will say, "Let us throw the whole thing away and get the same money by another tax" —a tax to which I had better not refer today.'

I meant—can you guess it?—a betting tax.

The clause was carried without a Division.

(2) *The Zoo-Clause*

But, a few minutes later, having stamped and trampled on the 'educational' principle, we picked up and petted it. I see with surprise that, only five pages later, I roared into action again: indeed, on that day, 19 June 1946, I made four speeches—and many 'interjections'—busy boy!

In his Budget statement Dr Dalton had said that he would fulfil his promise to amend the law relating to entertainments provided for a partly educational purpose by non-profit-making bodies. 'At present, exemption is allowed only if the Commissioners of Customs and Excise are satisfied that in each particular case the entertainment has educational value. I propose that in future the test shall be, not the educational merit of a particular play or a particular film, but whether the non-profit-making body which provides the entertainment has educational aims and activities.' (Vol. 421, col. 1826)

This affair has a tangled but entertaining history. There was nothing like it in the original Bill of 1916, which stopped short, for the most part, at stiff fences like 'wholly educational'—'charitable'—and 'philanthropic'. But on the Report stage (Vol. 81, col. 2146—17 April 1916) Sir George Cave moved to insert a new sub-clause at the end of Clause 1 (5):

'. . . or (*d*) that the entertainment is provided for partly educational or partly scientific purposes by a society or institution not conducted for profit, or is provided by any such society or institution, which has been founded with the object of reviving national pastimes.'

Sir George did not say a word in support of his amendment, and sat down. Sir F. Banbury said at once:

'I have been asked to inquire from the right hon. Gentleman whether botanical gardens will come under this Clause or not?'

Sir G. Cave said 'There may be exceptional facts but in most cases they would.' It is clear from earlier debates that the main thought and target of the Clause was *the Zoo*. In one of those discursive debates in Committee on 12 April there had been many questions about 'entertainments like the Zoological Gardens . . . where sometimes there is an additional attraction in the shape of a band or orchestra' (Sir W. Beale, Vol. 81, col. 1853). 'Will the myriad children who frequent those gardens be regarded as going there for educational purposes or for entertainment?' (Mr Boyton, Vol. 81, col. 1857) And finally Mr Montagu said, 'I will consider the addition of some words like "Zoological gardens not carried on for profit" or words to that effect.' Sir George Cave's amendment was evidently the fruit of Mr Montagu's 'consideration'.

In the brief debate on the new Clause, Mr Rawlinson asked (Vol. 81, col. 2147) what was meant by 'reviving national pastimes'? Would the Jockey Club come under that head? Sir George thought not. Others mentioned Eisteddfodau and swimming: but no one gave a thought to the theatre, the cinema, or music.

Mr Rutherford said severely (Vol. 81, col. 2148): 'We cannot get away from the fact that this portion of the Bill has not been thoroughly thought out', and, as they say, 'he had something there!' How, you may say, were the poor Ministers to tell what would come of their kind thought for the Zoo? How could they guess that, forty years later, their Zoo-Clause (as amended) would have a powerful influence on the dramatic arts and the theatrical industry? For myself, I know so well the fatigue that falls on all concerned in the closing stages of a complicated Bill that I am not going to throw any stones at the legislators who, without an amendment, without a Division, assented to the Zoo-Clause. But that does not excuse the continuance, and expansion, of accidental errors by later generations. I do not know what intelligent fellow first thought of employing the Zoo-Clause in the theatre, but the first application, I am informed, came from Sadler's Wells in 1934. Customs and Excise were dubious, but, 'on advice',[1] eventually assented: and so the trouble began. If it had been some 'commercial' fellow in the West End, the law, I expect, would have been amended at once.

In 1942, and again in 1943, Sir Irving Albery complained of 'tax-evasion' and a 'considerable amount of abuse'. (Vol. 379, col. 660) 'There has been laxity in giving exemption from this tax to theatrical concerns on the grounds that they are of educational or some other value. . . . There is nothing to prevent a person from drawing a very good salary and saying that his entertainment business is a non-profit-making concern. . . .'

On 19 October 1943 Sir John Anderson announced (in reply to a question from Sir Archibald Southby about Section 1 (5) (*d*) of the Finance (New Duties) Act, 1916) (Vol. 392, col. 1212):

'Sir Ernest Pooley, Sir Gerald Canny, and Dr T. H. W. Armstrong have been appointed as an advisory committee to assist the Commissioners of Customs and Excise in the task laid upon them of deciding what entertainments should be regarded as partly educational within the meaning of the Section to which the hon. Member refers. Directions have also been given that the Commissioners of Customs and Excise should take special care to satisfy themselves that every organization claiming exemption from duty under this Section is of a kind genuinely entitled to the benefits of its provisions. This will involve more detailed inquiry than in the past into the financial arrangements of bodies claiming exemption and into the disposal of the proceeds from exempted entertainments.'

But how surprising—and what a pity!—that that man of rugged sense, Sir John Anderson (now Lord Waverley),

[1] 'I rather think, after taking the opinion of the Law Officers of the Crown'—Sir John Simon, Vol. 326, col. 1344.

Chancellor of the Exchequer under another sensible man, Sir Winston Churchill, did not reply:

'The Section to which the hon. Member refers was intended to protect such institutions as the Zoo. It had nothing, and should have nothing, to do with the theatre, and in the next Finance Bill I shall take action to make that plain. . . .'

Many Parliamentary questions were asked about the new precaution. On 27 April 1944 Sir John Anderson told Major Lyons that since the appointment of the Three Wise Men '238 plays have been granted exemption from Entertainments Duty under Section 1 (5) (*d*) of the Finance (New Duties) Act, 1916. The number of plays refused exemption in the same period is 216.'[1] (So the censors at the Custom House had decided, roughly, on what some would call 'a 50/50 basis'.)

On 31 October 1944 Sir John Anderson, in reply to Professor Savory, said:[2]

'The following plays now running in London have been exempted from Entertainments Duty under the statutory provision relating to entertainments provided for partly educational purposes by a society, institution or committee not conducted or established for profit:

Hamlet.
Love for Love (Congreve).
The Circle (Somerset Maugham).
Richard III.
Peer Gynt.
Arms and the Man.
Scandal at Barchester (V. Wheatley's adaptation from Trollope).
The Breadwinner (Somerset Maugham).
The Importance of being Earnest (Oscar Wilde).
Charming Leandre (Th. de Banville).

[1] Vol. 399, col. 926. [2] Vol. 404, col. 626-7.

The Jubilee (Tchekov).
The Pariah (Strindberg).'

The Three Wise Advisers, it seems, compiled two lists of plays, A, the sheep and B, the goats. But even their devoted labours did not give general satisfaction: and on 25 January 1945 Mr E. P. Smith (Ashford, Conservative)—'Edward Percy', the playwright—asked the Chancellor:

'Whether he will take steps to end the invidious distinction between the A, partly educational and B, not partly educational, lists of plays furnished by His Majesty's Board of Customs and Excise in which the former are freed from Entertainments Duty when presented by non-profit-making companies while the latter are not.'

Sir J. Anderson: 'My hon. Friend will not expect me to anticipate my Budget Statement, but I can assure him that this subject is receiving constant consideration.' (Vol. 407, col. 984)

But what a pity—and how surprising!—that when the sacred Budget was disclosed at last Sir John Anderson, that man of rugged good sense, did not say:

'The more we try to apply the Zoo-Clause to the theatre, the more bogged we become, and the more ridiculous we look. Therefore, in the Finance Bill, etc. . . .'

Instead , in his 1945 Budget, he produced a new scheme, which, as a Budget Resolution, was carried. But, owing to the General Election of that year, it was not passed into law. This was the scheme which Dr Dalton took over and presented in 1946: and now it was welcomed by Mr Osbert Peake (Conservative), who had served at the Treasury under Sir John. 'At present,' he said:

'It has to be decided whether or not any individual performance is partly educational in character. We thus have the absurdity of having two lists of plays, films and so on, some of which have been held to be partly educational and some of which have been held not to be within the definition. *Charlie's Aunt*, I think, has been held to be a partly educational entertainment, and so has that rather bawdy 18th century play, Congreve's *Love for Love*.

'The proposal in the Resolution, as I understand it, is that the test in the future shall be the aims of the society producing the entertainment, and not the character of the individual show. *This is what was pressed upon us at the Treasury by the society representing authors, of which the hon. Member for Eton and Slough (Mr Levy) is a member and who came with other playwrights to the Treasury to press this point of view.* There will still remain, of course, the general test that the society producing must not be conducted for profit . . .' (Vol. 421, col. 2758)

Enter, thus, for the first time, my old friend and Parliamentary enemy, Mr Benn Levy, Member for Eton and Slough, and in my opinion the villain of the piece. This bearded, genial, sincere, able, and persuasive Socialist has had an immense influence in these affairs, and, I believe, a bad one. He is a fanatical supporter of the exemption of 'non-profit' companies (under the Zoo-Clause). Here, in his own words, is his gospel, as he expressed it that day:

'It has always been a fact that, fortunately, the theatre attracts a number of enthusiasts, a number of people who are anxious to do the best they can in the theatre, people who would be ready to work, and work well, regardless of profit. As I understand it, one of the purposes of this Resolution is to give encouragement to those people. This is a means of doing it in such a way as to avoid the necessity of discriminating as between play and play, and more or less avoiding the necessity—unless the point is unduly pressed—of discriminating as between one society and another. In other words, it avoids all the dangers existing in the law at the present moment in regard to discrimination; for discrimination means censorship. If the maximum emphasis is placed upon the elimination of loopholes for profit-making, then the question of whether societies are "partly educational" or not will answer itself, because people who are willing to forgo profit will presumably be more concerned with the cultural than the commercial aspect of the theatre.' (Vol. 421, col. 2762)

Later, on the Finance (No. 2) Bill, he said some sound words about 'partly educational':

'I regret that the phrase has been retained . . . because we may as well face it, that phrase means nothing or anything at all.' (It describes the Zoo pretty well.) 'It is quite beyond anybody's power to decide what play or what society is educational, . . . and, therefore, no play nor any spectacle could reasonably be excluded.'

(I agree with that, of course: but my conclusion is 'Scrap the whole Act which gave birth to the silly notion!')

'Forgo profits.' A word of explanation for those who have just 'tuned in' and may well be fogged by this affair. The heading to the Clause spoke of 'bodies which are not profit-making'; the Act itself of societies, etc., 'not conducted or established for profit'. Both are wrong: Mr Levy was right. The societies in question are very keen to *make* big profits, and some of them do. The point is that they are not allowed to *distribute* them. Except, I think, for the normal interest on capital invested, they must be 'ploughed back' into later productions.

In spite of all criticism the Clause still stands: and observe the stages in its extraordinary career:

(1) Stage One—1916—an afterthought introduced for the protection of 'partly educational' entertainments like the Zoo.

(2) Stage Two—1934—ingeniously applied—and dubiously granted—to a small theatre without doubt doing 'partly educational' work.

(3) Stage Three—some time in the 1940's—adopted by wealthy firms in the West End who operated ambidexterously—on profit-making plays through one company and

'partly educational' non-profit plays through another.

(4) (*a*) Stage Four—1946—the 'partly educational' test transferred from the play to the society presenting it—hence, *A Streetcar Named Desire* pays no tax.

(*b*) And now the Zoo-Clause is belauded as a great bulwark of the theatre.

Next (and it began in the same year, 1946) came

(5) Stage Five—when, not content with the privileges of the 'partly educational—non-profit'-folks, Mr Levy used them as an argument for retaining the tax on the main body of the theatre (see pages 71, 82, 136).

And that, you may think, as the ladies say, 'is the end'.

But it is not. There is, in the air only, another stage yet. This arrow was shot into the air by Benn Levy in 1946, and, in this mad affair, I would not bet that it will not one day hit the Statute Book. On 1 June 1956, Mr J. P. W. Mallalieu, M.P., shot a similar arrow:[1]

(6) Stage Six—We abandon 'partly educational' altogether and make 'non-profit-distribution' the only test for tax-exemption—the argument being (*a*) that 'partly educational' is silly, and (*b*) that people so keen to 'work for the theatre' that they care nothing for profit 'will presumably be more concerned with the cultural than the commercial aspect of the theatre',[2] and so will automatically produce partly educational plays. (Like *A Streetcar Named Desire.*)

But see how far they are getting from the Zoo-Clause. I never like comparisons between the drama and the dram: but all this is rather like saying to the famous Mr Fothergill, 'You enjoy running hotels and inns. If you promise not to "distribute" your profits, and content yourself with a salary, we will let you off the liquor-taxes.' What are the other hotel-keepers going to say?

More near the mark—what would be said if a similar scheme were proposed for newspapers and books?[3] The

[1] *New Statesman and Nation*, 1 June 1956.

[2] Mr Levy. Vol. 421, col. 2762. [3] See Appendix 'D'.

Minister responsible would be laughed out of public life—out of the country.

There were many questions about the new arrangements, for many Members did not seem to understand very clearly the new law which they had passed. Some wanted to know why companies which were exempt from tax charged the same prices as those which had to pay it. Dr Dalton replied that no requirement about prices was made by the Customs folk. (This, I think, is 'fair enough'. On the other hand it does not go very well with the deduction of 'tax-equivalent' from authors' royalties—see page 120.)

In 1949 there was a great fuss about the American play, *A Streetcar Named Desire*, which was presented at the Aldwych Theatre by H. M. Tennent:[1] Mr Geoffrey Cooper, Mr Marlowe, and Mr Wilson Harris all wanted to know on what grounds this play had been 'exempted from Entertainments Duty'.[2] 'Is the Chancellor aware', said Mr Marlowe,[3] 'that a vast body of opinion does not share his view that this play is in any way educational?' Sir Stafford Cripps patiently explained that he had never suggested that 'this play is educational': that the test was now different, the 'educational aims' of the society which presented it (22 November 1949). On 29 November, and again on 8 December, Mr Wilson Harris was after *Streetcar* and 'H. M. Tennent' again. On 8 December Mr Harris asked what is the nature of the association between the Arts Council of Great Britain and Tennent Productions Ltd. in the production of the play *A Streetcar Named Desire*—and the 'supplementary' questions filled three columns of *Hansard*. More than once Mr Levy came to the assistance of the harassed Treasury Bench:

'As the theatre in England is perennially hampered by want of capital, is it not highly desirable that it should be

[1] This famous and enlightened firm has two names—Tennent Productions and H. M. Tennent & Co. The first is 'non-profit'—the other is 'commercial'.

[2] Vol. 470, cols. 201-3, 941-3, 2082-6.

[3] Vol. 470, col. 202.

helped to capitalize itself in this way' (i.e. out of a play like *Streetcar*) 'on the sole and sensible condition that it refrains from dissipating its resources in the form of distributed profits?'[1]

The 'partly-educational-non-profit' scheme has done some good, I am sure (as any diminution of a barbarous tax must do) at Covent Garden, at Stratford, at the Old Vic and Sadler's Wells, at the lonely struggling repertory theatres in the provinces and the suburbs. Most of the symphony orchestras operate under it, I believe; and, so long as the tax endures, there may be something to be said for continuing to protect a privileged few.

But when it competes, in London or the big cities, with the ordinary honest-to-God tax-paying theatre, the competition is rightly considered to be unfair:

(*a*) the tax-exempt can continue to charge the same prices as the tax-payers: though sometimes they print on their tickets '12*s.* 6*d.* *including* tax', which seems misleading and even dishonest;

(*b*) though they charge the same prices to the public, as poor unfortunate 'non-profiteers', they wheedle their authors into accepting a deduction of 'tax-equivalent' from the gross before his royalty is paid;

(*c*) these, and other, advantages may give them £700-£800 a week; and with these resources they can afford to engage a row of stars, at high salaries, and yet secure much longer runs than the others, who, while still trying to recover their production costs, must pay many hundreds of pounds a week in tax—out of the till;[2]

(*d*) they can afford to pay for successful New York plays much higher terms than the tax-paying manager could face. (*Streetcar*, I have been told, was one example.)

On the other side, it is said that the tax-exempt, having made much money on a *Streetcar* (tax-free) can afford to put on more 'serious' or 'cultural' works. There may be

[1] Vol. 470, col. 942.

[2] *The Water Gipsies* paid £500 a week.

something in that—while the tax endures. But then, if there were no tax, *everybody* would have the same opportunity.

Again, who would listen if one talked in the same way about *The Times* and the *Sunday Slush*?

Personally, I should have been willing to let the Zoo-Clause alone while the tax remains. But, now that it is being pressed to the point of madness, I think it should be wiped out, tax or no.

TRIANGULAR DUEL

From 1945, when Mr Levy was elected, till 1950, when I was 'abolished',[1] there were three professional dramatists in the House of Commons, Mr Levy (Lab.), Mr E. P. Smith (Con.) ('Edward Percy'), and my humble self (Ind.). The House is always ready to listen to anyone speaking earnestly about any business which he knows well and most others do not. But when Mr Smith and I were making an impression, we thought, on all parties, and even on the Treasury Bench, Mr Levy would invariably follow and smoothly pour cold water on his colleagues: and there is no water so cold as that which falls from your own side. It was sincerely done, and courageously, for he was antagonizing, not only his own 'union', but, more important, the 'commercial' managers. But it was, I think, perverse: it was certainly damaging, for it gave the Treasury a happy excuse to sit tight.

On this day (19 June 1946) Mr Smith and I put down an amendment to the new edition of the Zoo-Clause, which I described, I see, as 'simple, logical, and beneficial'. It was certainly a good piece of drafting (I forget by whom) and I give it in full in case it can be used again:

'I beg to move, in page 4, line 36, at the end, to insert:

' "Entertainments duty shall likewise not be charged on payments for admission to any such entertainment, where

[1] University Member.

the Commissioners are satisfied that the entertainment is produced by a person, company, society, institution, or committee, whose object in producing the entertainment is partly educational, and that up to the date of such admission no profit has been made out of the entertainment by the producer: Provided that entertainments duty shall be charged on payments for admission after the date by which the Commissioners are satisfied that the excess of the total receipts over the total running costs of providing the entertainment is sufficient to recoup the initial production cost properly applicable to such entertainment." ' (Vol. 424, col. 277)

In other words, no tax to be payable till the production costs had been paid off.

I said, among other things:[1]

'The Clause to which I am moving this Amendment has a side note

' "Entertainments duty on certain entertainments provided by bodies which are not 'profit-making'."

'The motto of the Clause is, "No profit, no tax", and this Amendment is an endeavour to extend that principle up to a point to commercial managements which do not come under the Clause. I think it would be practicable to do that, although probably I shall be told that it is not.[2] Now, a play, especially a musical play, does not get on to the stage by itself. A great deal of money is spent before the play even begins. It may be that £5,000, £10,000 or £15,000 are spent. The other day I saw in a newspaper that a play cost £20,000—I think that must be exceptional[3] —in production costs before the curtain even rose.

'I have here some figures to show the Committee how very difficult it is even for a successful play to make money. The theatres are full, but everybody is not making a lot of

[1] Vol. 424, col. 278.

[2] C. B. Cochran said 'Yes'—some others 'No'. [3] Not now (1956).

money out of them. I have here the figures for two weeks of the Court Theatre, Liverpool. The play was not by some new upstart, not by some foreigner, but by the great Noel Coward himself, a very fine and, on the whole, successful musical show. In the first week the Liverpool public paid £3,698 to see this show; the Government took £1,044 by way of Entertainments Duty, and the production manager lost £408. The next week the public paid £3,956; the Government took £1,119, and the manager lost £366. In those two weeks, with a good show—I am told a very successful show, "capacity business", as they say, with even the matinées full—the Government took, by way of duty, out of the till £2,163, and the manager lost £774. How can one possibly conduct any business on that sort of line? . . .

(col. 279.) '. . . Let me take a more modest show in Glasgow. The public paid £2,063, the Government took £596 by way of Entertainments Duty, and the loss was £34. That was not an expensive production. The plays go round the Provinces. It is very difficult to make money in the Provinces nowadays, because very often one cannot pass on the Duty by raising the cost of the admission tickets. The plays struggle on. They come to London. They have still a terrific burden on the production bill to pay off; in addition, they have to make a profit on the running expenses each week.

'What I propose is that no duty should be charged until the initial outlay, the production cost, has been paid off. It is a simple thing. A week after the show begins, the manager can produce his production account and show what he has spent on buying dresses and this, that, and the other thing, on the producer's fee, and so on. That account can go to the Customs and Excise, they can examine it, they can, if they like, say it is too much and they cannot pass it, and thereafter, the account can be made. When the production cost has been paid off, the Entertainments Duty can be charged. The day after that the show may start making a loss, but I do not propose helping the producer any more then. I say he should be given a chance to make a profit before the Government take these huge sums of £1,000 a week. That is the proposition. My hon. Friend the Member for Eton and Slough (Mr Benn Levy) may say that the rapacious bricks and mortar men take all the money. There may be things to be said about them, but if there are, the problem must be dealt with in some other way. We are now talking about the producer, the creative manager, who takes the risk of putting these plays on the stage, and although he does not have the privilege of the people mentioned in the first part of the Clause, while he is not making a profit, should have this benefit.'

The Member for Ashford, Mr E. P. Smith, as always, made a lively and persuasive speech (Vol. 424, col. 281):

'. . . I have been delving into certain records and I compute that the little brain of the hon. Member for Ashford has enriched His Majesty's Treasury during the course of its working career in the shape of Entertainments Duty to the tune of £300,000; while the greater brain of the hon. Member the Junior Burgess for Oxford University has probably enriched His Majesty's Treasury in the shape of Entertainments Duty to the tune of half a million of money, and probably more. Therefore, we do not present ourselves before the Treasury today as necessitous mendicants praying for alms. We stand before the Treasury as important customers demanding a traders' rebate. . . .

'. . . I want to conclude upon a more serious note. The theatre is the one industry above all others which has the greatest ups and down. It supports a large number of men and women—I am not talking about stars—who have a very hard and hazardous struggle to live. They are people by whose side uncertainty and anxiety as to the future always walk. We all know, as a symbol, the clown who laughs and dances and capers when his heart is breaking. That is a symbol; but it is true today to say of the men and women who are players that they rarely have a period free from anxiety through the whole of their lives—a tremendous anxiety as to their future which, if it is at all possible, should be made safer and more secure. Players, men and women alike, are gallant, gay, infallibly generous, eager to help any good or kindly cause. As my hon. and learned Friend the Member for Exeter (Mr Maude) said so movingly in the House the other night, the theatrical profession is indeed an honourable occupation. What I am pleading for is that the Treasury should make it a little more safe, and secure. They have it in their power to do so.'

Up jumped Mr Benn Levy at once (Vol. 424, col. 283):

'I am very sorry to find myself opposing my two colleagues on this issue. I am sorrier still to be about to antagonize those interests upon whom I depend for my bread and butter, by opposing an Amendment which I have little doubt they will welcome. . . .

(col. 284). '. . . I ask whether there is any advantage to the theatre. Does it really help the theatre? Quite definitely, it would help the speculator. I cannot see that it would help the theatre to be more vital, or more vigorous, or to develop more freely or more experimentally. It would cut the losses to the investor, and I am certainly not against that. On the contrary, I favour a reduction of losses in the theatre provided, and this is important, that winnings in the theatre are kept inside the theatre. That is the effect of the Clause as it now stands without the Amendment. That is why it is such a particularly good Clause, because it links up the exemption of Entertainments Duty with the stipulation that no profits are taken out. That may have an enormously beneficial effect on the theatre in the long run, for instead of the theatre having to go cap in hand to the speculator and the City when money is wanted to produce plays, it will have an opportunity, through this Clause, of building up its funds and of being able to finance itself. . . .

'. . . The Amendment will torpedo the Clause to the detriment, and not to the benefit, of the theatre. It will torpedo the Clause for the simple reason that if people are given the alternative, which this Amendment would provide, and are told in effect that they can either not take any profits out of the theatre and obtain exemption from Entertainments Duty, or that they can obtain exemption from Entertainments Duty on their losses but still take profits out of the theatre, the net result can only be an enormous bias in favour of the second course.'

Mr Levy, it seemed, thought the amendment 'practical' enough.

The Solicitor-General, Sir Frank Soskice, a delightful person, and as a rule a persuasive speaker, evidently did not know much about the thing. He 'adopted' Benn Levy's argument, but also made some heavy weather about the 'practical difficulties':

'It would be quite impracticable and would need an enormous staff. It would be impossible to ensure any sort of accuracy in the collection of the tax. . . .'

Mr E. P. Smith: 'They could make returns as they do now. . . .'

Mr Kenneth Pickthorn (Cambridge University) was very good (col. 289):

'. . . I cannot resist the feeling that the Solicitor-General was precisely and completely mistaken on every line he took and on every point he made. . . .

'. . . He made two principal points. One was that there could be no reason to differentiate between the theatre and the cinema. . . .'

(col. 290.) 'The cinema does sometimes, but very seldom, contribute some idea or method to the theatre. Not, I think, very often. It is not very often that the theatre desires to adapt the cinema script for its purposes. And it is not very often or for very long that the theatre desires to exploit for its purposes personalities which have been built up in the cinema. But the cinema is continually under obligation to the theatre, to the theatre of the last 2,000 years; and every month as the months go by it is again and again put under obligation to the theatre. It is from the theatre that the cinema get ideas and suggestions and gets, in the main, persons.'

And, later on, on the 'partly educational' stuff, he said (col. 290):

'. . . I would ask the Committee to consider whether we really have lived long enough under this régime, by which one kind of entertainment or one kind of diffusion of ideas is encouraged by the State by differential taxation, to be sure that it is really a good system in the long run. All my prejudices would be in the opposite direction. I should always be prejudiced in favour of the theatrical entertainment which was instituted and put upon the boards by an individual because he thought that enough of the public would like it to enable him to make a profit; I would always prefer that and would encourage that rather than encourage the entertainment which is put upon the boards because a lot of elderly gentlemen and ladies think that the stuff which they were brought up to believe was improving would be good for the young. . . .'

I became a little hot, I am glad to see, and roared into action again:

(col. 292) 'No speech that I have ever heard has made me more determined to divide the Committee, if I can find anybody to go into the Lobby with me, than that of the learned Solicitor-General. He asked what would be the situation if this Amendment were passed. Let us consider what will be the situation if it is not passed. You will have these shows on one side of the street under this education rigmarole. We are to have these theatres run by societies, institutions or committees . . . whose objects and activities are "partly educational", whatever that means. I understand from hon. Members opposite that the words "not conducted or established for profit" mean that the profits from one enterprise are dug into the next one. But, strangely enough, that has been precisely the practice of those low fellows, the commercial managers, for the last 500 years, those base fellows who are so impudent as to wish, not merely to give the public education, enlightenment, and entertainment, but to provide new hats for their wives and to take their families to the seaside in August.[1] Those are the people who, whether they win or lose, pay a tax of 40 per cent. On the other side of the street, paying no tax at all, there will be people who provide no more education than people like Mr Cochran. . . . This is a matter of justice. It is ridiculous to say that any men who make a profit out of the theatre are bad men. The point is, it is a bad thing to put a tax on turnover when people are making losses. That is the simple issue. . . .'

The Committee divided: Ayes, 103; Noes, 275.

1947

In 1947—a year later, almost to a day—there was another, and still more surprising performance of 'When Dramatists Disagree' (Vol. 438, col. 1611). The rates were still at the war-peak reached in 1943, when the theatres were packed. On 16 June I put down a new Clause to reduce the rates to the pre-war level of 1939—that is, by a half—on the 'living theatre' (which, in fact, was done by Sir Stafford Cripps in the following year). This was a most important and illuminating debate, and beautifully illustrates the difficulties of those who fight for the theatre in Parliament.

[1] I treasure a brave story about the late Sir Charles Cochran. He had had two or three successive 'flops', and was finding it difficult to raise money for his next production. He had a great many French pictures—especially by Toulouse-Lautrec—of which he was very fond. He summoned a famous picture-dealer to the house in Montagu Street, and said, 'I want to sell some pictures. Have a look round.' The dealer 'looked round', and said, 'Which pictures do you want to sell, Mr Cochran?' 'C.B.', said, 'I want £10,000 for a new show. Take any of the pictures that add up to £10,000.'

The State was now taking 4*s*. 8*d*. on a 16*s*. stall, leaving the management 11*s*. 4*d*. We modestly proposed that we should go back to Sir John Simon's level of 1939 when the State took 2*s*. 6*d*. and left the manager 13*s*. 6*d*. Yet we were defeated—by the fanatical Benn Levy and the Zoo-Clause. Mr E. P. Smith and I filled 16 columns of *Hansard*. I select a few passages which are necessary to follow the course of the debate and may be historically helpful. I said, timidly (Vol. 438, col. 1613):

'Any tax upon receipts is questionable, but a tax on receipts upon what is the most speculative of all human activities must be bad in itself. The production of plays, concerts, recitations, variety shows, is not like selling a packet of matches or a bottle of whisky, something for which the demand is certain and about which there is very little difficulty today. Here no man can command success, a hundred causes over which he has no control may take it away. I remember many managerial post-mortems in the past, at which we agreed that nothing is good for the theatre. Bad weather is bad for the theatre, and very good weather is bad for the theatre.[1]

'When the sun is shining people want to play tennis, and, when it is wet and cold, they would rather stay at home and read a book. Again, before a holiday, they are saving their money for their holiday, and, after the holiday, they have no money left. In times of national mourning, they do not feel like going to the theatre; in times of national rejoicing, the Government puts on State processions, parades, and firework shows free of Entertainment Duty, or an industrial exhibition. Indeed, we used to decide that there are only two good days for the theatre in the whole year. One is Christmas Day and the other is Good Friday, and on both of those days the theatres are closed.

'There are other factors to take into account. The tenor

[1] In 1953 Mr R. A. Butler, justifying the total exemption of cricket, said: 'Cricket is subject to the vagaries of the weather.' (Vol. 515, col. 2037)

may develop laryngitis, or the baritone may fall under a bus, or an actress may go off and have a baby. In my last show[1] it happened that both leading ladies, after three months, went off—bless them—to increase the population.[2] There are other hazards over which the producers have no possible control, and yet this is the industry on which the Government decide to levy a tax upon receipts. . . .'

('I see that here and there I refer to a 'tax of 42 per cent', which may be misleading, for the top tax on the gross takings, from 1943, was about 30 per cent. But I meant—as Mr Osbert Peake described it—'40 per cent on the price of the ticket clear of the duty.')

(col. 1615) '. . . Let me add this, although I suppose I need scarcely remind the Chancellor of this fact. We have here an exportable product. I do not know what the British theatre and British actors have earned in dollars during the last few years, but the amount must be very considerable. A year or two from now it may be very difficult to sell a British motor car, but we shall still be able—at least, I hope so—to sell British plays and books. But we cannot export British plays unless they are based upon a healthy and prosperous home industry. Nobody would have thought of bringing over here the famous play *Oklahoma* unless it had had a very long and successful run in New York. . . .'

'. . . . . . I am authorized to give a few figures about Mr C. B. Cochran's last production but one,[3] which was seen by many Members of this House, including Mr Speaker and the Serjeant at Arms, neither of whom, apparently, considered the author should be committed for contempt, although it dealt with the proceedings of this House. It was a light musical play, but it had a sort of "message", it paid respect to our institutions, and particularly to this place. (AN HON. MEMBER: "Who was the author?") I have been humbly trying to avoid bringing

[1] *Big Ben.* [2] And see page 129. [3] *Big Ben.*

that up. He is one of the hon. Members for Oxford University. That play went on tour for ten weeks and played to a packed house everywhere it went. It gave a great deal of pleasure and, although I say it myself, I think some little inspiration to many large audiences. During those ten weeks the public paid £39,000 to see the play. Of that, the management handed over £11,000 to the State. (AN HON. MEMBER: "Hear, hear.") Yes, but at the end of that ten weeks' successful tour, not merely had the manager made no profit, but he had lost money. Does the hon. Member still say, "Hear, hear"? The cost of production of that play was about £12,000. If the manager had been allowed to keep in his pocket £11,000—I am suggesting in my Amendment that he should keep only £5,000—he would, at least, have been able to pay off something of his production costs.'

Mr John Paton (*Norwich*): 'Is the hon. Member arguing that the total cost of production should have been borne by the provincial tour?'

Sir Alan Herbert: 'Not at all. I am saying that if one entertains people in five provincial capitals for ten weeks, it is a curious thing if one comes back to London with no profit at all, having handed over to the State the sum of £11,000. That seems to be a fairly simple proposition. However, we came back to London. There we "went very big" indeed, in July. The play went just as big as *Oklahoma* has done. Seats were booked up for months, and for 15 solid weeks the public paid £5,800 a week to see this play. Of that sum, the State took £1,700 leaving £4,100. The running costs weekly were £3,000. The cost of production was £11,000 or £12,000, and a simple calculation will show that the manager had to work for 11 or 12 weeks before he got back the cost of production and could begin to make a profit. Is that not an astonishing way of doing business? We carried on, with all the hazards, including those of leading ladies having babies and tenors having laryngitis, and eventually after 31 weeks of successful entertainment the play came off. During all those months the public had paid £154,000, of which the State took £45,000, and the management lost, I learn today, £4,000. Is there anybody in the world who would like to carry on a business on those terms?

(col. 1618) 'If I may give one more example of the way in which this business is being conducted, let me quote this one. This is about a gentleman who does not wish his name to be mentioned publicly. But I got the information, lest I had the figures wrongly, in a letter from a chartered accountant about the yearly earnings of this particular man, who is a very good man in the theatre—not a playboy who bounces in to make money, but a good man of the theatre, a respected manager. During the year ended 31 May 1947 he paid out in salaries to artists £89,000; he paid to the State Entertainments Duty of £68,000; he made a loss of £17,000. I hope that what I am driving at will now be clear to hon. Members.

'The point is that people cannot possibly run business on those terms. They do go on. How do they go on? They seek more and more the line of least resistance. They tend more and more to bring over established successes from New York—most of them very good, but not so good as all that. Less and less are they ready—I do not blame them—to take the risk of producing new British plays. So we have people like Mr Priestley knocking at the door year after year with plays, interesting plays which are not certain of success, to be sure, but which ought to be produced.

'I am glad indeed to see my hon. Friend (Mr Benn Levy) here, because he is a very respected member of the dramatic world, a very fine playwright. I am sorry he has not put down his name in support of my new Clause. I think I know the reason he has in mind. He is in favour of the non-profit arrangements set up under the Finance Act last year. I say nothing against him. But I very much doubt their working. I wonder whether these arrangements are going to lead to much creation—to creative activities in the theatre. I am rather afraid that the non-profit-people are very likely to go to the non-copyright, non-royalty-earning plays like those of Shakespeare and Congreve, and to opera, and that sort of thing. Certainly, those arrangements are doing good, because it will be quite impossible to produce more opera if it has to pay Entertainments Tax. But I wonder, are they ever going to produce anything to stand up to *Oklahoma* and those other big American musical plays, for example? *It is rather important that we should stand up to them. Big Ben* cost £12,000 to produce. There is another play whose name I will not mention—I do not want to advertise[1]—that cost £15,000 because prices of everything have gone up. I wonder what non-profit-making person is going to put money on that sort of thing, especially if he is told that, while there is no profit for him, the management are going to get no more than £25 a week.'

(I did not then know that such plays as *Bless the Bride* would never be allowed under the non-profit arrangements).

'Surely it is not the intention of the Government to drive what is called the commercial manager out of business altogether? Or is it?

'I shall very soon hear somebody say, I know: "It is all rents. It is all a question of rents." If it is a question of the rents that are charged for theatres, then I hope the Government will do something about it. But I think there is a great deal of exaggeration of this question of rents. First, if I accuse the Government of taking £1,700 out of the till every week of a theatre, it is no answer to say that that is right because the man who owns the theatre has taken £500 out of the till. The man who provides the theatre has a right to something. He has taken a risk: he has provided something. Whereas the State has done nothing and provided nothing and has no obligations. . . . I have been looking into the matter. I am told that the number of the rapacious rentals that are charged can be counted on the fingers of one hand. Certainly, as I know, the lessee who is on "sharing terms", as they call it, has obligations. He has in some cases got to

[1] *Bless the Bride.*

provide staff for the whole theatre, the house staff, the box-office staff, the stage door people. Or, in other cases, he has got to pay his ground rent, local rates and water rates and insurance, which may run into £2,000 a year. Indeed, the cost of the upkeep and maintenance of a large theatre may be something like £15,000 a year. If that is the case it is not surprising if high charges are made for the use of theatres, especially as the owners have got to take the risk of the theatre being left empty on their hands. . . . However, my main point is this. If there is anything wrong about that, it is for the Government to deal with. In the meantime, here is my new Clause, which deals not with rent, but Entertainments Duty. . . .

'There are two major musical mysteries in history. One is the old question, what song the Sirens sang. The other is: Who wrote, and who composed, the song in the Chancellor's heart?[1] . . . I should like to think that he went to a British author and a British composer; something produced by some modern man of British enterprise . . . a song with which I had something to do:

"I want to see the people happy."

I am sure that in the last analysis that is the song in his heart. And so I wish that he or some member of the Treasury had been attached to poor Mr Cochran on the very day that the preparation of that particular play[2] began, and had watched all the troubles and difficulties from first to last. I wonder whether at the end of those proceedings he would have said: "Now this is an industry which ought to bear a special tax of 40 per cent"? . . .

'Sir, it is a very proud and stirring thing for anybody associated with music or the theatre to stand on one side when the people go out and to see their happy faces—if the show is successful—to hear them say that for two or three hours they have been taken out of themselves, refreshed and

[1] Dr Dalton. [2] *Big Ben.*

relaxed, and have forgotten their troubles, politics, and all the rest of it. But when they have all gone it is a very sad thing for the manager to look at the figures, even when the whole place has been packed, and to realize that the whole of that elaborate and most difficult edifice may be founded financially on quicksand, not because of anything inherent in the structure, but because it is being undermined by the State—which, God knows, wants to see the people happy as well as we do—simply because the State, in its folly, I think, has thought fit to impose a tax of 40 per cent upon those who cater for the happiness and enlightenment and spirit of the people.'

Mr E. P. Smith said a few straight words about the 'non-profit' affair (col. 1625):

'Last year, non-profit-making companies were freed from the obligation to pay Entertainment Duty, provided their entertainment was partly educational, which included all entertainment—since even bad entertainment is partly educational; it shows you how not to do it. It is severely educational in that respect. An enormous number of non-profit-making companies have subsequently sprung up. . . .

'The Board of Customs and Excise take the greatest possible pains—and rightly so—to ensure that those concerned with the management of non-profit-making companies do not make any secret profits, and that the profits, if any, are ploughed back into the venture, which was the object of the League of Dramatists when they prevailed upon the then Chancellor of the Exchequer to exempt genuine non-profit-making companies from the Entertainment Duty. The Board of Customs and Excise have no power to supervise contracts or expenditure. Non-profit-making companies are therefore in an extraordinarily favourable position compared with the purely commercial managements. Speaking as a dramatist, I would far rather have a play of mine produced by a non-profit-making company, than by a commercial management, not because I should receive more royalties, because my trade union—although we are legally free to do so if we choose—has come to a gentleman's agreement with the non-profit-making companies that they shall not be charged more than we should have received from a commercial management. But because, with that wonderful 28 per cent to 34 per cent in hand, a non-profit-making company has a greater chance of standing up to the common vicissitudes of the theatre. Expenses are *ipso facto* a lighter risk; and there is every chance that a play will run longer and keep the author's pot boiling for a greater period of time.

'We must question whether that is quite fair to the commercial managements . . .'

Then, once more, up got our colleague, Mr Levy:

'Although I have no doubt at all that they believe that this new Clause is in the interests of the theatre, I am persuaded that it is exactly on those grounds that the Committee ought to reject it, namely that it is, in fact, against the interests of the theatre.'

(Yet this earnest man had a play running at the Wyndham's Theatre at the time, presented by a 'commercial' manager.)

He said, as usual, that only the landlords would benefit from any relief (which proved, the following year, to be quite untrue), and then, as usual, urbanely deflated us with the Zoo-Clause (col. 1629):

'But even if this were not true . . . the new Clause is . . . out of date. . . . For what happened last year? The Chancellor produced a Clause in the Finance Bill which completely and wholly exempted managers from that tax if they chose. *There is now no obligation on any manager to pay any Entertainment Duty at all.* (AN HON. MEMBER: "On what terms?") I will come to that in a moment. The Junior Burgess for Oxford University asks merely for a reduction of the Entertainment Duty to the prewar level. But in fact nobody need pay anything. There is one condition attached. Anyone who wants to be exempted from paying the tax has simply to undertake to plough the profits back into the theatre. But that is precisely what everybody who is interested in the theatre, and who loves it, wants to happen. We want people to plough profits back into the theatre. We want to build up a large financial reserve with which the theatre can finance and support itself. . . .

'The hon. Gentleman said that Mr Cochran made a loss on a very successful show.' Why, said Mr Levy, did Mr Cochran not take advantage of the Zoo-Clause? 'If he had, instead of losing £4,000 he would have had £45,000 in the bank. It is true that the £45,000 would have had to be devoted in putting on other plays, but that is precisely what Mr Cochran likes doing, and what we want him to do. Where the difficulty arises, I honestly do not understand. . . . I feel that the arguments are overwhelmingly against this Clause because what the Chancellor said in his last Budget —whether he knows it or not—to the managers was in effect, "Here you are, here is a preferential tax on all managers who are unwilling to keep their profits in the business." I want quite frankly to keep that preferential tax.'[1]

Mr Christopher Hollis finely supported us (col. 1631): '. . . If it were merely true that the theatre was suffering under two staggering blows—one a bad system of rents, and the other a bad system of Entertainment Duty—the fact that the rent problem still remains to be dealt with, and could be dealt with along the lines suggested by the hon. Member for Ashford (Mr E. P. Smith), would not be an argument against also dealing with the problem of Entertainment Duty. . . .'

He went on to the Zoo-Clause, and said:

[1] But why should the theatre alone be singled out for this extraordinary device? What would be said if a similar 'preferential tax' were proposed on the producers of newspapers and books?

'The question we have to face in dealing with the Entertainment Duty is not whether the non-profits system as a whole is a bad system which ought to be condemned—which I do not think anyone would maintain—and I certainly would not—but whether it is now possible to do without the commercial theatre altogether.

'The Junior Burgess for Oxford University (Sir A. Herbert) has raised a point that certain kinds of plays which would be highly desirable in the public interest should be produced, but are not likely to be produced under the system as it is at present—the non-profit-making system—and the hon. Member for Eton and Slough to some extent agreed with that. . . .'

In fact, of course, Mr Levy's frequent suggestions that Sir Charles Cochran (and my humble self) could, and should, 'go non-profit' were spurious. I say it with regret, but they had great effect on the House. None of the 8 pieces I wrote for Sir Charles would have been admitted by the Customs and Excise into the sacred area of exemption (see pages 126-127). And there was more to it than that, as I spluttered in an extempore reply. Cochran, justly or not, described the whole thing as a 'racket' and would have nothing to do with it (col. 1641):

'There is no reason why a man like Mr Cochran, who has served the theatre for fifty years, should be limited to £25 a week. That is a condition of the non-profiteering racket. It is in many ways a racket, and that is one reason why Mr Cochran and people like him are against it. It is not merely a question of ploughing money back into the business. The real managers have been doing that all their lives and long before the hon. Member came here.'

Dr Dalton (the Chancellor) said (col. 1635):

'*If all the playwrights had been unanimous*, it would have been easier for me to reach a decision: but the fact that my hon. Friend the Member for Eton and Slough (Mr Benn

Levy) considers—and gave good reasons for so considering—that the acceptance of this new Clause would be against the interest of the theatre which we all desire to forward makes my position a little difficult.'

He was very friendly—suggested a 'working party' on the theatre—but 'I do not think I can take off nearly £3 million extra here, particularly in view of the doubtful consequences which the acceptance of this new Clause would produce' (col. 1640).

Mr Osbert Peake (Leeds, North), leading for the Conservatives, spoke strongly for our proposal (col. 1642):

' . . . The hon. Member for Eton and Slough (Mr Levy) feared that all the benefit of a remission might go to the landlords. My own view is that that would not happen, and that any remission of taxation on the living stage is bound automatically to be divided between the management, the public and the employees of the theatres. (HON. MEMBERS: "No.") If that is not the case, then of course there is no argument at any time for a reduction in the tax upon any commodity. It will always be argued that if a tax is taken off a certain article, such as a motor-car, the benefit will not go to the public or to the management but to the landlord. That would be a good argument against any reduction in taxation.

'The hon. Member for Eton and Slough also referred to the fact that by becoming a non-profit-making society any manager could avoid the payment of Entertainment Duty, but if he will refer to the Section produced in the Finance Act last year which re-enacted the old exemptions with some slight differences, he will observe that only a limited class of living stage performances are covered by the exemption. For example, the music-hall does not come within the definition of Section 8 (1) of that Act. . . .'

But the mischief had been done. The Committee divided: Ayes, 99: Noes, 206. (col. 1646)

Another victory for Mr Benn Levy.

1948

SIR STAFFORD CRIPPS

That autumn poor Dr Dalton had to resign—and Mr Nigel Birch, who had been hunting Dr Dalton for a long time, made his indignant and classic complaint, 'My God, they've shot our fox!'

Sir Stafford Cripps succeeded him, and in his first Budget speech (Vol. 449, col. 73) he said:

'I now come to the question of incentives. Since 1935 a distinction has been drawn between the living theatre and other kinds of entertainment; and in 1946 sports—other than racing—were added to the list of entertainments which were eligible for the reduced scale of tax. I believe that we should encourage these forms of living entertainment, particularly the theatre; and I propose, therefore, to increase the measure of relief from duty which they already enjoy. For theatres, concerts, circuses, sports, and other entertainments which at present qualify for the reduced rates, payments for admission up to 1*s.* will be exempt from duty, and the duty on payments above that amount will be approximately half the present rates.''[1]

This took the theatre back to where it was before the war (roughly 15 per cent) and to rates about twice as high as the original rates of 1916. But it was, nevertheless, a very welcome relief. Sir Stafford Cripps took his place beside Mr Neville Chamberlain and Sir John Simon in the theatre's list of heroes. Mr Levy did not say a word: nor, for that matter, did Mr E. P. Smith or I say the tiniest 'I told you so'.

Sir Stafford also gave some special relief for entertainments in rural areas (see The Twelve (or Thirteen) Exemptions—page 102).

[1] As I suggested (for the theatre) in 1947. Rate (1948—living theatre): 1*s.* + 0*d.*; 6*s.* + 1*s.*; 10*s.* 6*d.* + 1*s.* 11*d.*; 12*s.* 6*d.* + 2*s.* 4*d.*

LOCAL AUTHORITIES—MR A. BEVAN

I must mention, too, Mr Aneurin Bevan's Local Government Act of 1948: for Clause 131, which was an afterthought (popped in on the Report stage), has some relevance to our theme—or should.

The Clause was entitled 'Provision of entertainments', and it empowered local authorities to provide 'an entertainment of any nature', to provide 'a theatre, concert hall, dance hall, etc.', to 'maintain a band or orchestra' and do anything 'incidental to the matters aforesaid', including refreshment—up to a rate of 6*d.* in the pound.

The Clause was not favoured by the Conservatives, but Mr E. P. Smith welcomed it 'on behalf of dramatists, actors, stage-hands and,' he said, 'the commercial production managements and the "non-profit-making companies" '—though he expected opposition from the "bricks and mortar men" ' (who own the theatres).

There was much to be said for it, though much that was said for it was, as usual, incautious, boastful and unnecessarily offensive.

'It is clear,' said Mr Edwards (Labour), who moved the Clause, 'that private enterprise is either unable or unwilling to deal with the expanding cultural needs of our people . . . I have the conviction that if the local authorities are given these powers they will help to deal with the relative cultural poverty of the Provinces, and that they will put private enterprise entertainments very much on their mettle.' (Vol. 447, col. 1347)

As I remarked later (col. 1808), it was unfair to say that sort of thing without adding that the State laid a penal tax of 29 per cent on the receipts of those unfortunate people which would not be paid by the local authorities.

But who can blame the Parliamentary Secretary, for later (col. 1382) his own Minister revealed a startling ignorance of these affairs. 'There is,' said Mr Bevan, 'in this country, to a very remarkable extent an intellectual and artistic renaissance.' He told a merry tale about a group of Welsh miners who 'made large profits' out of running a cinema which they nobly ploughed back into the institute to buy books for the library.

'The committee were very angry because they were called upon to pay Entertainment Tax. They asked me to intervene to see whether this tax could not be removed. I said that *if they had made a profit* they had to pay the tax. They said "How are we to avoid the tax?" I said "Fail to make a profit", and they said, "How do we do that?" I said, "Devote every fourth week to providing a celebrity concert, or what might be called an unprofitable high-brow entertainment to raise the general standard of education." They put on *Medea* and several other Greek plays. In three weeks' time' (quick work!) 'I had another letter calling my attention to the fact that it was no good because they had made more profit than ever.'

Sir W. Darling: 'Entertainments Tax is not paid on profits: it is paid on the tickets. I am sorry to spoil the Minister's story.'

Mr Bevan: 'It is the same thing.'

Happily, it is not given to all men to know everything: but when one hears the rulers speak with such airy ignorance of the delicate affairs into which they are putting their well-intentioned feet, there must be, among those who all their lives have been engaged in such affairs, some slight diminution of the spirit.

The Clause was opposed, but carried, by 255 votes to 76.

On Third Reading I supported the Clause but, by request, expressed the reservations of the theatrical world: and, I am glad to see, I had a go at 'commercial'. . . .

'I was somewhat surprised when I heard the hon. Member for Ashford list among the people who were in favour of this proposal what he called the "commercial" production managers. I prefer to call them professional production managers, because "commercial" is a word of prejudice.

We do not talk about commercial publishers, or commercial newspapers, or commercial films, although they all have to pay their bills and make both ends meet. Curiously enough, in spite of the undoubted reforms which His Majesty's Government have introduced, so far as I know there has not been any amendment to the laws of bankruptcy. Therefore, it is very unfair to throw such epithets as "commercial" at anybody merely because he is trying to pay his bills. . . .

'I have received a communication from the Theatres National Committee, which comprises several bodies; they are the Society of West End Managers, the Theatrical Managers' Association, the Entertainments Protection Association, the Provincial Entertainment Proprietors' and Managers' Association, the Association of Circus Proprietors and the Association of Touring and Producing Managers. I do not know what half of them mean, but they are not all "bricks and mortar" men; they comprise the producers and everything. I do not know whether they are right or wrong, but, as a matter of record and of justice, I must tell the House what they say. They say: "This Committee takes strong exception to the new Clause tabled by the Minister of Health with regard to the above matter." I shall not read the whole letter. But they go on to say: "The theatre managers do not wish to adopt a dog-in-the-manger policy or to discourage the provision of opportunity for theatrical entertainment in places where it is not adequately provided at the present time"—

'That is the point I have made, and there I am absolutely with the writer of this letter—

"but they feel that in a matter of this kind considerable care is needed if irreparable damage is not to be done to the best interests of the British theatre in the long run."

'In other words, we shall not substantially increase the intellectual resources of this country if we drive out Mr Cochran and substitute the mayor and corporation of Wigan or Swindon. . . .

'. . . What I am saying is that these powers should not be

used too automatically. Where there are theatres already in existence and where it seems that the public demand is adequately supplied, there should be consideration and consultation. I am sure the theatrical managers are not afraid of fair competition.

'Subject to that, I add my humble blessing to this Clause. In many ways, it is a great feather in the cap of the mummers, the long-haired authors, the painted ladies and so on. It is good to know that our works and our wares are appreciated so much. I am glad that so much emphasis has been laid on the theatre, my enthusiasm for which, I believe, is shared by the Minister. . . . I do not care how far the synthetic glories of the radio and the films are developed. They may go on until we have a television set in every bathroom and we can smell the perfume of the beautiful blonde upon the screen, but I swear that even then there will never be such a thrill as the sound of a great orchestra tuning up in the sight of the citizens before a great concert, or, better still, perhaps, the lights going down in the theatre as the band begins before the lowered curtain, and there sit the people, socially gathered together—it is the most sociable and civilized of all public entertainments—to hear the speech of living actors in all the plays of the world, while behind in the long corridors is heard that ancient, historic and exciting cry, "Curtain up!" If the right hon. Gentleman can indeed find means of communicating that thrill to thousands of citizens who have never known it, I think that his name may be a thousand times blessed.' (Vol. 447, col. 1813)

But, in fact, I gather, neither the hopes of Mr Edwards nor the fears of the Theatre have been confirmed. Local authorities have not rushed into the cultural battle. A few, especially at seaside towns, have provided orchestras, and other holiday 'attractions': but fewer than 20, I believe, have done anything for the theatre—even for the 'non-profit' companies. This is a pity. The local authority's aid for a struggling repertory would be a much healthier way out than the fictional 'tax-equivalent' arrangements which are discussed later (see pages 120–123).

1950

In 1950 there were big doings in the cinema world, and the temporary tax of 1916 gave birth to a new monster, more strange and complicated than the Zoo-Clause. This was the Eady Levy,[1] which, if I understand it aright, is a wonderful way of robbing Peter to pay Paul. But let the industry tell the tale in their own words:

BRITISH FILM PRODUCTION FUND LTD

'The history of the Fund commences in 1950 when in the Finance Act certain concessions in Entertainments Duty as applicable to cinemas were granted. It had previously been agreed within the trade as represented by the four Associations[2] and with the Treasury that conditional on such concessions being forthcoming exhibitors would contribute certain levy payments to a central fund. It was the agreed intention that such fund should be used for the support and encouragement of the production of British Films. Contributions to the Fund by exhibitors were to be made at the rate of ¼*d.* for each seat sold at gross prices exceeding 3*d.* Cinemas exempt from Entertainments Duty and cinemas which in any week took less than £125 gross were not liable to make levy payments.

'The above arrangements were to continue for one year from 10 September 1950, but as a result of further discussions and adjustments to the scale of Entertainments Duty

[1] After Sir Wilfred Eady, who acted for the Treasury.

[2] i.e. The British Film Producers Association, The Cinematograph Exhibitors Association, the Kinematograph Renters Society, and the Association of Specialized Film Producers.

contained in the Finance Act, 1951, agreement was reached on an extension of the levy scheme for three years from 5 August 1951. For this period the rates of levy were ¼*d.* per seat sold at gross price 4*d.* to 1*s.* inclusive and ¾*d.* per seat sold at gross prices in excess of 1*s.* The exemptions from liability to make levy contributions continued as previously except that as from 30 December, 1951, the figure of £125 relative to gross weekly takings was increased to £250.

'The existing scheme, which runs until October 1957, and which also makes provision for marginal relief, provides for levy payments at the following rates:

Gross Admission Prices	*Levy*
Up to 8*d.*	Nil
9*d.* to 1*s.* inclusive	¼*d.*
1*s.* 1*d.* to 2*s.* 2*d.* inclusive	½*d.*
2*s.* 3*d.* to 2*s.* 6*d.* inclusive	¾*d.*
2*s.* 7*d.*	1*d.*
2*s.* 8*d.* and upwards	1¼*d.*

'Payments to the Fund by exhibitors are not treated as taxable receipts in the hands of exhibitors and it is agreed that in the case of films hired on a percentage basis amounts paid by way of levy are an allowable deduction from receipts before the calculation of film hire.

'During the first four years of the Fund the following accounts have been collected by way of levy:

47 weeks to 4 August 1951	£1,197,666
52 weeks to 2 August 1952	£2,971,910
52 weeks to 1 August 1953	£2,732,726
52 weeks to 31 July 1954	£2,750,518

'As regards the distribution of the fund a scheme was agreed between the four Associations and approved by the President of the Board of Trade in March 1951. Subject to a few amendments the same scheme continues to operate and will remain in force during the extended period of the levy until October 1957. Briefly the scheme provides that in each year the monies collected by the fund are to be distributed to the producers of eligible British films shown during the same year subject to the prior payment of administrative expenses and any monies allocated for "other purposes" to which reference is made later. In general terms the amount or portion of the fund distributed in respect of each film is based on the amount of film hire earned by such film during the year; such amount or portion bears the same ratio to the distributable total of the fund as the film hire earned by such film has to the total film hire earned by all eligible films during the same period. Films of which the registered length is 3,000 ft. or less received more favourable treatment than longer films in that the amount of rentals in the case of the former are multiplied by two and a half times before allocations from the fund in respect of the same are calculated.'

I may be mad, but this sounds to me like putting a high tax on books at the book shops but giving some of it to the publishers. But the Scheme was highly thought of, and, I believe, has benefited the British film producers (see page 150—The Cinema Case).

1952

MR R. A. BUTLER

In 1952 (Mr R. A. Butler in charge) there was a new turn of the screw. Racing (which had been taxed at the same rate as the film) came down: other sports (football, etc.), which since 1947 had kept company with the theatre, went up to join horse, dog and motor-racing. So now there were three different rates, as there are today (God knows how many there will be when we go to press!). They are set out fully in Notice No. 1 by the Commissioners of Customs and Excise—enormous lists from which I have extracted a few examples:

	Charge to Public		Duty		Amount retained by Proprietor	
	s.	*d.*	*s.*	*d.*	*s.*	*d.*
(1) On the living theatre, ballet, concerts, etc.	5	0		8	4	4
	7	0	1	0	6	0
	10	0	1	6	8	6
(2) On racing, games, sports, etc.	5	0	1	4½	3	7½
	7	0	2	0½	4	11½
(3) On the cinema	5	0	2	4	2	8
	7	0	3	3	3	9
	10	0	4	8½	5	3½

So, if you had a 10*s.* ticket at the cinema, the State took 46 per cent of your money: and, though my main brief is for the struggling theatre, I regard that as barbarous. On a ten-shilling book, quite rightly, you pay no tax at all.

For the year ending 31 March 1955, the cinema tax yielded £35,330,000, 'Sport' paid £3,250,000, and the theatre about £2,170,000.

(The 'Sport' figure is made up thus: Horse-racing £926,000, dog-racing £530,000, speedway racing £65,000, football £1,350,000, boxing £105,000, other racing and sports (including motor-racing, wrestling, swimming, and God knows what) £272,000.)

1953

In his 1953 Budget Mr R. A. Butler was responsible for two more 'mutilations'.

(A) He exempted 'amateur sport' as well as amateur drama, and amended the law about the latter. The Clause (5) was discussed in Committee on the Finance Bill on 19 May 1953. (Vol. 515, col. 1973)

There was a lively debate, not about sport but about musical conductors.

The definition of an 'amateur performance' in the Act of 1949 said that the amateur status was lost 'if any payment is made or reward given for the appearance of any of the performers whose words or actions consitute the entertainment or any part of it, or for any person's services in connection with the entertainment as instructor, producer, manager or conductor or in any advisory capacity'.

Mr Butler's new Clause (1953) conceded that 'a paid instructor, producer, manager, or adviser' might be permitted.

Mr Rhodes (Labour) now moved—I am deliberately piling up these dreary details to show you how much toil, and trouble and time is devoted nearly every year to feeble nibbles at this foul and ridiculous tax—Mr Rhodes moved an amendment (Vol. 515, col. 1985) to insert

'. . . or as a conductor, or member of an orchestra taking part together with other persons in the entertainment.'

This suggestion, whether sound or not, was of great practical importance. The least effective amateur performance can be endured if the band is professional, or at least laced with professionals. But if the orchestra is squeaking discordantly and out of time the suffering is entire and continuous.

Mr Rhodes said that the concession would cost only £10,000, and (Vol. 515, col. 1987):

'Does the hon. Gentleman believe that amateur performances compete with professional performances? I do not think that anyone could possibly argue that they do. . . . It may be argued that the advent of the local amateur dramatic society in the local theatre or local hall might do some damage to shows put on in adjacent towns, but we know that that is not so.'

I do not know how Mr Rhodes knows that. 'The village hall' may do no damage: but I have heard from many a professional touring manager how badly they can be hit if they happen to clash with the local amateurs' weeks, which the whole town loyally attends.

It was, perhaps, with such thoughts in his mind that Mr Maudling clearly gave the Treasury view:

'The principle on which we have worked is that it shall be an amateur performance if none of the people participating in the performance is paid . . . the same principle that we are seeking to apply in the case of sport. . . . There are those who actually participate and those who are essential for the putting on of the entertainment or sport, and without whom neither can be put on, though they do not actually participate. . . .

'. . . If all the people who participate in the performance are amateur, then it is an amateur performance, but if anyone participating is paid then the line is crossed and the amateur concession has to be lost. . . .' (Vol. 515, col. 1992)

The amendment was lost by only 4 votes—Ayes, 268: Noes, 272.

Cricket

(B) Hooray! The tale grows crazier and crazier, for, having thus exempted amateur sport, and insisted on total-amateurism in amateur drama, Mr Butler, in the next Clause (6) (Vol. 515, col. 2005) went on to exempt cricket matches, which may be played entirely by professionals.

Cricket clubs, I suppose, are nearly all 'not for profit' societies; and cricket stands so high in the national esteem—'a wholesome influence in the moulding of character', etc.—that I always wondered why the M.C.C. did not apply for exemption long ago on the ground that they and their 'entertainment' were 'partly educational'. But they never did: and it was left to Mr R. A. Butler to put cricket on the highest level, next to the 'wholly educational', for the game would be exempt even if you put it on 'for profit.'

'In most sports,' said Mr Butler (Vol. 514, col. 55, 14 April 1953), 'the amateur definition which I have devised will, I think, work reasonably well, but it will not do for cricket. In this country cricket occupies a special place among sports, not only as forming part of the English tradition but as a common interest helping to bind together the various countries of the Commonwealth.'

Unlike the plays of Shakespeare and A. P. Herbert—or lawn tennis, or golf.

The Chancellor's salute to cricket was not supported with the automatic and general reverence which he may have expected. Mr Gaitskell moved an amendment (Vol. 515, col. 2005):

'To leave out "cricket matches" and to insert "All entertainment which consists of games or other sports".'

(Pause for a moment, reader, before we go on, and consider how great, how fantastic, a wonder it is that the British Parliament should be compelled to debate such small but obviously unanswerable questions! Ask yourself too—what kind of minds must they have at the Treasury who by their mean distinctions and invincible obstinacy compel such childish discussions?)

Mr Gaitskell reminded the Committee that in 1952 his Party 'had objected to the increase of the duty on sport. We objected to it on the two grounds: first, that it would create financial difficulties for a great many sports clubs of different kinds up and down the country, and, secondly, because we could not see any ground for discriminating in favour of the live theatre and against sport. We still hold strongly to that opinion.'

Mr Gaitskell did not 'object to the exemption of cricket' (Vol. 515, col. 2008), but he did find it difficult to justify. He mentioned the Rugby League. 'Test Matches are played in Australia and New Zealand.' He mentioned soccer, and commented amusingly on the Chancellor's remark that 'cricket is part of the English tradition'. (Vol. 515, col. 2009)

'That was not a very convincing argument. We know that the word "tradition" makes a special appeal to the Conservative Party. It really means that the older a thing is the more they are in favour of it. . . . The Chancellor should look up the facts on this and see just how cricket and football stand in relation to each other. The results of my researches show that football is a great deal older than cricket. It was played in some form by the Greeks and Romans. It was played in London in 1175. It was forbidden by Edward II in consequence of "the great noise in the City caused by hurtling over large balls". It was again prohibited by Henry VIII because, I understand, of the "brutality and violence associated with the game."

'After this splendid record in our island history I am afraid that cricket cannot bear comparison. As far as I know. it was not until the reign of Edward IV that cricket was prohibited—several reigns after the time when football was prohibited. . . . The truth of the matter is that we may say that cricket is our national summer pastime. But the fact is that football is our national winter pastime, and the Chancellor is discriminating against the winter sport. I can understand the attraction of summer sport, but when we come to taxation the argument should surely be the other way. It is very attractive to play or to watch games in the summer: it is much less attractive in the winter when it is windy, wet, cold, snowy and frosty. Winter sport should be helped rather more than summer sport. . . .

'The Chancellor will say . . . that cricket is in a very difficult position, that clubs are losing money, attendances are falling, and so on. I really must tell him that precisely the same thing is happening in other sports. . . . I cannot see how he can possibly defend his special treatment of cricket while leaving all other sports to bear the higher taxation which he imposed last year.'

Nor can I. Every good Englishman was glad in his heart about the cricket privilege: but logically there is nothing to be said for it. It makes nonsense of the Act to which it has been added, like a clown's hat on a clergyman. It should be the last nail in the tax's coffin.

Many other 'sports and games' put in a plea. To think, I say again, that, year after year, our industrious Members should be condemned to debates like this!

Mr Edelman spoke for professional tennis. Mr P. B. (Laddie) Lucas (Brentford and Chiswick) spoke for golf,[1] especially the Open Championship which is 'financed on a non-profit-making basis', but, as in cricket, the players are both amateurs and professionals.

Mr W. T. Proctor (Eccles) spoke on behalf of the game of bowls.[2] The balance of the Lancashire Professional Bowling Association, he said, had 'gone down from £550 to £309'. The four players received only 4*d.* each game, and it was hard that they should lose their amateur status—and exemption—for so small a sum.

Mr J. P. W. Mallalieu (Huddersfield, East) objected to 'all attempts to discriminate between various sports' and especially to 'the discrimination between amateurs and professionals'. Why not, for example, exempt professional football? 'What the Chancellor is now doing is to encourage the worst features in professional football by forcing these clubs to continue the transfer system which, in my opinion, is wholly wrong. . . .'[3]

Mr R. J. Taylor (Morpeth) said: 'The Committee have been talking about golf, tennis and other "classy" sports, but I want to talk about foot-running.'[4]

Mr Ronald Bell struck a new note:[5] 'Cricket, I think, is in a different position, because it is not an entertainment at all. According to one's attitude towards it, it is either an inspiration or a soporific.' You may laugh, but that, I understand, is the private attitude of the Commissioners of Customs and Excise (see page 106).

Mr R. A. Butler made a long and patient defence of his plan. Everyone had asked him to do something about cricket, and now he had, why all the bother? 'Cricket has to be played,' he said, 'over a long period, and is subject to

[1] Vol. 515, col. 2023. [2] Col. 2024. [3] Col. 2030.
[4] Col. 2032. [5] Col. 2032.

the vagaries of the weather.' Mr Gaitskell protested again that he was not anti-cricket but pro-sport-exemption: and the amendment was defeated by 267 votes to 256.[1]

The next day (20 May 1953) there was another long debate on Mr Ellis Smith's amendment to insert after 'cricket' the words 'and football' (cols. 2100–190), and after that another on Lieutenant-Colonel Bromley-Davenport's amendment to insert 'and boxing' (col. 2189).

According to a memorandum from the Football Association (quoted by Mr Ellis Smith)[2] Mr Reginald McKenna double-crossed them, as well as the theatrical managers:

'Entertainments Duty was first levied on Association football in 1916. The then Chancellor of the Exchequer assured the Football Association that this was only an emergency measure, and he asked the Football Association to enlist the support of the clubs to carry it into effect. . . .'

As usual, the Treasury spokesmen made no reply to this allegation. The Financial Secretary (Mr John Boyd-Carpenter), indeed, seemed to think that the tax, like wine, had acquired merit through age:[3]

'. . . We are dealing with a state of affairs which has lasted for 37 years, and while, of course, that is not conclusive . . . it is perhaps a little bit material . . . to recall that this is not a new impost. . . .'

Mr Adams said:

'. . . The Chancellor by his changes—and other Chancellors must accept their responsibility—has worked himself into a complex and impossible situation. . . .'[4]

But Mr Butler was quite serene.[5] There appeared in his speech, for the first time, I think, something called 'The New Entertainments Tax Structure', which is the three-tiered arrangement I have already described. He mentioned it many times and related its history in racy terms.

[1] Col. 2040. [2] Col. 2103. [3] Col. 2132.
[4] Col. 2152. [5] Col. 2180.

His predecessor, Dr Dalton, it seems, had got into a muddle about the tax:[1]

'... When I came along I succeeded a most dreadful row and revolution on the subject of speedway racing, in which the right hon. Member for Leeds, South had been submitted to the most obscene form of pressure groups—from his own supporters—ever known in this country.

'Happily for this country he now sits on the other side of the Committee. The right hon. Gentleman attempted to stand up to that pressure as best he could and he did so with considerable energy. He was like a fox pursued by the hounds, and at length he reached his lair only by covering his own scent by saying that he would institute an inquiry into the matter. That inquiry is what I found on assuming office after his untimely "death". I also found the mangled remains not only of the right hon. Gentleman but of the Entertainments Duty structure. I therefore proceeded to readjust the duty not according to the lines I necessarily thought right, but on lines which were in response to the inquiry and what had gone before. Having accepted those lines, I naturally took responsibility for them, which is all I could do.

'The result of that inquiry was that a new group, which included sports, was set up in the centre of the Entertainments Duty structure. The right hon. Gentleman and his friends are now proposing to put a bomb under the new Entertainments Duty structure and remove from it the sport which provides the main amount of duty. If the Committee insist on that procedure going through tonight they will deal a very serious body blow—we are coming to boxing very shortly—against the Entertainments Duty structure as a whole. Frankly, I could not stand for such a step being taken tonight in the way suggested by the right hon. Gentleman. It would have an effect upon all the other revenue we get from Entertainments Duty, and that would be wrong....'

[1] Col. 2181.

And later:[1]

'... I must confess that I need the revenue which comes in from the football duty. I regard it as an integral part of the structure of the duty as a whole, and I think that there are clubs who can afford to pay, if we are to have any Entertainments Duty at all. ...'

When I read all this, I said to myself (indeed, I wrote it down), 'We are going to hear much more about the new "Entertainments Duty Structure". The Treasury are afraid. Each meritorious "concession" leads to others—or, at least, to demands for others—and long debates. Very soon, there will be no tax at all. But, if we erect a solemn Structure, we can resist any amendment, not on its merits, but because it would interfere with the Structure.'

(You will be amazed to hear that I was right—see Vol. 555, col. 350: 'We cannot monkey about with different parts of the Entertainments Duty. If we make changes at any point we must review the duty as a whole ... extend our survey to the whole structure.' Mr H. Brooke, Financial Secretary, 26 June 1956.)

The amendment was rejected by 278 votes to 261.

For the very interesting debate on the boxing amendment,[2] see Vol. 515—20 and 21 May, 1953—beginning at col. 2189. Dr Summerskill and Mrs Braddock played lively parts on opposite sides. The Tax Structure won.

THE 12 (OR 13) EXEMPTIONS, ETC.

As we go to press, the 'Exemption and Repayment Provisions' number twelve (or thirteen including cricket), and the latest list is as follows:

[1] Col. 2184.

[2] Mr Jack Solomons writes: 'The Entertainments Tax has crippled most boxing shows. My estimated losses since it began ... have been in the five-figure class.'

(1) *Indoor Entertainments in Rural Areas*

Section 17, Finance Act, 1948, as amended by Section 11, Finance Act, 1949.

This was a Cripps benefaction. To get it you have only to satisfy the Commissioners of Customs and Excise that the entertainment is held in a building situated in a borough, urban district or rural parish within the meaning of the Local Government Act, 1933 (or, in Scotland, a small burgh within the meaning of the Local Government (Scotland) Act, 1947, or a landward parish, or the landward part of a parish partly landward and partly burghal), with a population not exceeding 2,000 or with a population not exceeding 640 to the square mile—and that seating capacity for more than four hundred persons cannot be provided in the building. For this purpose, by the way, you tricksters, a building does not include a building not attached to permanent foundations.

(2) *Wholly Educational Entertainments*

Section 1 (5) (*b*), Finance (New Duties) Act, 1916.

Yes, this is one of the veterans. Here you have only to satisfy the Commissioners that your entertainment is 'of a wholly educational character' (no bother here about profit). You do this by writing a letter to the Secretary, H.M. Customs and Excise, King's Beam House, Mark Lane, London, E.C.3., who is the big authority on education. You may ask me what you say in your letter. Do you say, 'This play is by Shakespeare—or A. P. Herbert'? Or do you describe the plot of *Hamlet*—or *Bless the Bride*? Do you say, 'This is a concert of music by Handel'? Or must you describe the music of the master, and estimate its effect upon young children? I cannot tell you. But, if there is any argument, it will be settled by the Ministry of Education (or, in Scotland, the Scottish Education Department).

(3) *Schools, etc., Entertainments*

Section 12, Finance (New Duties) Act, 1916, as amended

by Section 8, Finance Act, 1921, and Section 12, Finance Act, 1923.

Careful here. No profit: sole purpose of promoting some object in connection with the school, institution, or organization, and all the performers must be receiving or have received instruction in the school, institution, etc.

Get hold of Form ED.23 from the nearest Customs officer, when he is not chasing smugglers.

(4) *Entertainments provided by Partly-Educational Organizations*

Section 8, Finance Act, 1946, and Section 3, Finance Act, 1952.

This is the Zoo-Clause, as amended. Two things (*a*) 'not for profit', and (*b*) 'aims, objects, and activities' of your society 'partly educational'.

On (*a*) the Commissioners will want to know about your financial arrangements with the owners of the premises and with the performers. And you can't go shares with 'profit-making organizations, or with individuals'. Controlling chaps must be 'financially disinterested'. On (*b*) be careful. The test is no longer, 'Is this play partly educational?' but 'Are your aims, etc., partly educational?' Nevertheless, you must give the Commissioners details of each programme for which exemption is sought. They will 'have regard to your choice of works taken as a whole. Exemption may be allowable for an *occasional light work* provided that the activities of the society over a period are acceptable when taken together as evidence of compliance with the terms of exemption.' *But note*—you are forbidden 'a music-hall or other variety entertainment'. Does this include 'revue'? No, it seems, for revues have crept in. A 'stage-play' is all right—but, *quaere*, is an 'occasional light' *musical* stage-play?

(5) *Partly Scientific Entertainments*

Section 1 (5) (*d*), Finance (New Duties) Act, 1916.

Another of the veterans, and still intact in its original shape. That is, it will not be enough for the Royal

Geographical (or Astronomical) Society to say that its 'aims and objects' are 'partly scientific'. It must show that each entertainment deserves that title, and there is nothing here about 'an occasional light work'. A frivolous exhibition by the Royal Society will have to pay the tax.

'Not for profit'—as in (4).

(6) *Revival of National Pastimes*

Section 1 (5) (*d*), Finance (New Duties) Act, 1916.

Another veteran—part two of the Zoo-Clause. Here I can think of nothing but Morris dancing and archery. But, if things go the same way in the theatre much longer, we may see one day a gallant manager claiming to put on a play under Exemption 6.

'Not for profit'—as in (4).

(7) *Amateur Stage, etc., Entertainments*

Section 10, Finance Act, 1949, as amended by Section 7, Finance Act, 1953.

'Not for profit'—as in (4).

Form ED.59. Note—you may pay for the services of any person as instructor, producer, manager, or in any advisory capacity. But if you pay a conductor, or any member of the orchestra, you're done (for reasons, see page 95: but then see Exemption 13, Cricket).

(8) *Amateur Games or Sports*

Section 7, Finance Act, 1953.

This was a Butler benefaction. Form ED.60, 'addressed to the appropriate Collector of Customs and Excise'.

'Not for profit'—as in (4). No 'payment or reward' to performers. But 'prizes of a reasonable number and value' are permitted.

(9) *Exhibitions, Shows, etc.*

Section 11, Finance Act, 1923, as amended by Section 7, Finance Act, 1924.

This is a terror—and a long one too. The best thing is to write to the Secretary (as above—(2)) at once. But I will try to give you the form briefly. You must be 'Not for profit', as in (4). That settled, you can get exemption for a wonderfully mixed bag of exhibitions—ranging from the products of an industry (including agriculture, horticulture and the breeding of animals of ANY description—except, I suppose, rabbits), to works of graphic art, sculpture and arts craftsmanship (or a mixture of them) executed and exhibited by persons who practise graphic art, sculpture and arts craftsmanship for profit (shame!) and as their main occupation, or of displays of skill by such persons in such arts and crafts, or, if you like, articles or displays of skill which are of material interest in connection with questions relating to public health.

But take care that you don't allow any 'dutiable items' to slip in and corrupt your status—the vocal concert, for example, at the flower show is dangerous, as we have seen. Amusements, though, which are not of a kind liable to duty, 'for example swings', will not get you into trouble. Then, if you madly propose to present a gymkhana, you must study this with care: '*Gymkhanas, etc.*—Jumping competitions and riding and driving competitions *may* be admissible where they are tests of the qualities of the horses' (but where, you may petulantly reply, are they not?) 'or where they are displays of skill in riding or driving by workers in agriculture'. (Engage Pat Smythe, and you are done—or aren't you?) 'Horse-races, which are ordinary sporting events, musical rides, trick-riding, tent-pegging and similar displays are not admissible under this provision.'

Isn't it fun?

(10) *Entertainments Promoted by Permanent Charitable Bodies*

Section 6 (4), Finance Act, 1924.

Form ED.40. You must be a society 'of a permanent character' (no doubt the form will explain that). 'The whole of the net proceeds' (which means 'the difference between the receipts and the expenses of the entertainment') 'must go to philanthropic or charitable purposes'.

(11) *Entertainments the whole takings of which are devoted to charity*

Section 1 (5) (*a*), Finance (New Duties) Act, 1916.

No expenses, however small, to be taken out of the takings, or out of the charity's kitty.

(12) *Entertainments the net proceeds of which are devoted to charity*

Section 1 (5), Finance (New Duties) Act, 1916, as amended by Section 6 (4), Finance Act, 1924.

Form ED. 13.

This is a repayment, not an exemption provision. You pay the duty and get it back later—if you can.

(13) *Cricket Matches*

Finance Act, 1953.

Cricket is not mentioned in the official document I have before me (Notice 100). This, I wickedly suspect, is by Treasury instruction, for, in 1952, rejecting some amendment, Mr Butler said: 'If we were to make differentiations of that sort we should rapidly upset confidence in the structure of the tax' (Vol. 500, 6 May 1952). Cricket, prettily perched on the top of the structure, does make the whole thing look pretty silly.

There are no regulations, they ask no questions, and you have to fill up no forms. You can, if you like, make and 'distribute' profits, and play teams of professionals only. If it's cricket, it's all right.

A courteous letter from Customs and Excise says that 'cricket matches are excluded from the entertainments which are subject to duty'. But a humorous officer said privately, 'The fact is that cricket is not counted as an entertainment.'

1954

In 1954 Mr Butler faintly reduced the rate (see Appendix 'B').[1] But on 25 May the vigorous Mr Woodrow Wyatt (Labour) moved a new clause proposing to abolish the tax on living performances. He was supported by Members of all parties, Mr J. E. S. Simon, Dr Barnett Stross, Mr Anthony Crosland, Colonel Lipton, Sir Robert Boothby, Mr S. Silverman, Mr Beverley Baxter, and Mr Glenvil Hall. He was opposed by Mr Gerald Nabarro and Squadron-Leader A. E. Cooper.

Mr J. Boyd-Carpenter, Financial Secretary, remarked that the amendment, if accepted, would cost £1½–£1¾ millions: and he told an astonished House that the tax had been in existence since 1916.

1955

In January 1955 the Theatres Entertainment Tax Committee issued this admirable challenge:

THE FUTURE OF THE BRITISH THEATRE

To all Those Whom It Ought To Concern

From the days of Shakespeare the British theatre has not only enriched the life of the nation, it has extended a benign and civilizing influence over the European and English-speaking peoples throughout the world. Of all the arts and industries of entertainment throughout the land it is the oldest and most characteristic of our culture. It has produced, and still produces, a stream of writers, performers, and craftsmen with inherited skills. It constitutes a rich and unique tradition.

2. But now all over the country our theatres are closing down. Famous playhouses, local repertories, Victorian

[1] Rate (1954): 1s. + 0d.; 6s. + 11½d.; 10s. 6d. + 1s. 10½d.; 12s. 6d. + 2s. 3½d.

music-halls—new and old—are putting up their shutters or being given over to different purposes. Dozens of others, not yet closed or closing, are struggling on against repeated losses. Almost every year fewer companies of players tour the country with fewer plays. There is a present danger that the art of the theatre will disappear, except in a few big cities. Even the London theatre, which draws its audiences from a vast urban area and from the rest of the world as well, is restricted in the scope and variety of entertainment which modern circumstances permit.

3. The continual increase in the cost of everything has hit the theatre more hardly than any other craft or industry. For by its very nature the living stage cannot increase its output—an actor can only give so many performances in a week and a theatre can only hold so many people. It is not even allowed to open on Sundays. Moreover the theatre, unlike many other industries, cannot pass on to the consumer the rise in its costs without fear of driving its audience away. Its only remedy is fewer productions with smaller casts and single sets.

4. But even more important than rising costs is the rising competition which now faces the theatre from other forms of entertainment: first, the cinema, then the radio, and finally television. One performance in a television studio may be watched by seven or eight million people, the performer on the average stage is lucky to be seen by five hundred. As the television network has spread over the country, more and more local theatres have been put out of business.

5. But the living stage is not only the parent of all these other kinds of entertainment. It is, and must always be, their recruiting centre and training ground. The Theatre, and especially the local theatre, is the school in which the talents of performers, playwrights, and dramatic technicians are discovered and developed. Without a vigorous and flourishing theatre the other dramatic arts must soon decline.

6. Under such conditions the living theatre is no longer

able—should no longer be asked—to bear the burden of paying Entertainment Duty. The theatre does not ask for subsidies, though even some theatres which are subsidized still run at a loss. It only asks that at long last this intolerable incubus be removed. By all means let the theatre sink or swim by its own unaided efforts, but let us not sit by and watch it being scuttled by a tax which was always unjust and has now become lethal.

7. This is the old story of a tax imposed in wartime—in this case in 1916—for the duration of the emergency, and then kept on year after year despite the sympathetic regrets of successive Chancellors. Even if there was a case for subjecting entertainments to a special duty, the form of the tax is as unfair as it could be, for it is levied on losses and profits alike. No matter how big the flop or how great the losses, the tax must still be paid on every ticket sold, and it works out at about 15 per cent of the total Box Office takings.

8. So harshly has this tax borne upon the living theatre that in Budget after Budget the Chancellors have been obliged to grant an ever larger range of exemptions. Without these exemptions, the plight of the living stage would be even worse than it is. But despite all these exemptions—and the anomalies they have created—by far the greater number of theatres are still compelled to pay the tax. The time has now come for tax on living theatrical entertainment to be altogether abolished.

9. The yield of the tax is less than £2¼ million a year—only ·05 per cent of our annual budget of some £4,000 million. But that £2¼ million will make all the difference to the theatre. For many it will constitute the marginal 15 per cent between survival and disaster. It will reduce losses all round and convert some losses into a profit, thereby enabling many a hard-pressed concern to carry on. It will increase the opportunities for employment and lead to better conditions in every branch of the theatrical industry. In the big cities it will encourage managements to be more venturesome and experimental with new plays, new authors,

new techniques. In short, the removal of the tax will give a tremendous and well-needed stimulus to the vitality of our national theatre, which is an asset we ought jealously to preserve.

10. Confronted by the present crisis, the organizations directly concerned with the well-being of the theatre have formed The Theatres Entertainment Tax Committee for the purpose of urging the immediate withdrawal of the Entertainment Duty upon theatrical entertainment. This Committee seeks the support and assistance of all those who have the interests of the British stage at heart.

1953

'NO FINE ON FUN'

On 30 April 1953, at the Royal Academy Dinner, I had had the great honour to reply for the guests and propose the health of the President, Sir Gerald Kelly. Among other things, I said, I think without irrelevance, certainly without shame:

'The Prime Minister had an easy task. He had only to answer for Her Majesty's Ministers. I have to answer for the Opposition as well, and for all the contending eddies of Art and Politics that swirl about this peaceful table. The Prime Minister will know, as First Lord of the Treasury, that this great Exhibition is one of the rare "entertainments" which are exempt from Entertainments Tax. It ranks, in fact, with cricket in the Culture Handicap, and well above the Leicester Galleries. Well, we propose to go farther. We propose to abolish Entertainments Tax entirely.

'NO TAX ON THOUGHT! NO LEVY ON LAUGHTER! NO DUTY ON BEAUTY! WHO TOOK FIFTY MILLIONS OFF THE PEOPLE'S FUN?

'What a cry! What a just and noble cry! All this boasting about "Full Employment"! After 2,000 years of Christianity, and Socialism, and Science, is that the finest carrot we can set before the toiling asses—that all should be able to *work*—

all the time? No, Sir, anyone can work—we all like work—and we are rightly taxed for this indulgence. But when we have done, when we go forth to enjoy the finest things that Man can make or do, the things that distinguish us from the savage and the sheep, whether it be fine writing or painting, fine music or singing, or fine riding on a fine horse, then it is barbarous to tax us as if we were enjoying some dangerous narcotic or intoxicant. No, Sir, "Full Enjoyment" is the cry. And that, Sir, is the policy of all the parties, all the arts, all the guests for whom I speak tonight.'

After the banquet I said to a Conservative Minister, then at the Treasury: 'Well, I hope you do it. If not, I bet you the Labour Party do.'

Sure enough, at the General Election of 1955, first the T.U.C. and then the Labour Party, in their Manifesto, declared for 'the abolition of the Entertainment Tax on sport and the living theatre'.

Some Conservatives described that part of the Labour manifesto as a piece of 'opportunist' vote-catching, and I felt it just to defend our old supporters (in *The Times*):

'. . . I wish to be fair to all. It is unfair to say, as some do, that the Labour promise is "mere electioneering". On 26 June, 1940, I see, I wrote in your columns: "Those who took most part in the long fight to get the music and drama tax abolished or reduced were on the Government side; but we always found our best and warmest supporters on the Labour benches." So it is not, in those quarters, a "new idea". It would be equally unjust to say that Conservatives today have no interest in this reform. On the Order Paper in the last Parliament stood a motion for abolition signed by 161 members of all parties, 70 Conservative and 89 Labour. Both Sir Winston Churchill and Mr Attlee were vice-presidents of the Stage and Allied Arts League, which was formed for the express purpose of liberating living entertainment from the duty.

'So it is a non-party affair, and should remain so. . . .'

When I read the news, I said to myself, I remember, 'At last, we have no more to fear from Benn Levy, for he can hardly go against his own party.' What folly! True, there were no more public speeches or letters on the subject. But it was madness to count him out: and the strange tale that follows is, at least, an interesting example of the power that one determined man can acquire behind the scenes, simply by working hard and being on the right committees. It should also be a lesson to the rest of us, who, convinced of the justice of our cause, are content, sometimes, to write angry letters to the papers and let others do the dull committee work.

V

The Battle of 1956

MR HAROLD MACMILLAN

No one is compelled to read it all: but I am going to tell the story of the Battle of 1956 (the theatre's battle) fairly fully. At the end of it all we may seem, on paper, to have got no more than a few kind words from the Chancellor. But we had, as well, defeated, only just in time, some deadly internal enemies. These, when opportunity serves, will strike again: and therefore I put the whole intrigue and argument on record. Then, the people of the theatre may be glad to know how strenuously their leaders and representatives have served them: and all should know what mountains of toil and trouble are required to extract a small kind mouse from the Chancellor of the Exchequer.

For all I know, the cinema, the sports and other corners of 'entertainment' have similar stories: but all I can do for them is to give their own 'statements of case', which I do on pages 150 to 158.

[1]

15 May was the fortieth anniversary of the collection of the tax. But it was a year of exceptional hope, and promise, in this prolonged struggle:

(*a*) The 'case' was stronger than ever. On pages 138–146 you will find the excellent statement that was sent to the 358 Members of Parliament before the Committee stage of the Finance Bill, which could not be bettered. Costs of production were soaring up. A great new rival —Independent Television—went into action in the autumn of 1955, and (during a great drive for savings) was subsidized by the Government. On the screen of the B.B.C. Mr R. A. Butler and his men said 'Don't spend', and on the I.T.V. (with Treasury aid) little men said, more persuasively, 'BUY BLOTTO'.

(*b*) The theatre had an excellent organization. In November 1954 my old Parliamentary colleague, Mr Dingle Foot, Q.C., a man of ability, charm and judgement, became the chairman of the new Theatres Entertainment Tax Committee (set up by the Theatres' National Committee). On this body almost everyone interested in the theatre is represented—not, for special reasons, the Society of Authors and Composers, but we have sent 'observers' from time to time, and agree with the Committee in its main purpose—abolition.

There are the Association of Circus Proprietors of Great Britain; Association of Health and Pleasure Resorts; Association of Touring and Producing Managers; British Actors' Equity Association; British Drama League; Concert Artistes' Association; Musicians' Union; National Association of Theatrical and Kine Employees; Scottish Theatrical Proprietors' and Managers' Association; Society of West End Theatre Managers; Theatrical Managers' Association; and Variety Artistes' Federation. The deputy chairman is Mr Joseph Dean, and the secretary Lieutenant-Commander C. C. Powell, R.N., known for years as a skilled Parliamentary agent.

(*c*) Through their persuasive activities and documents 358 members of the House of Commons—more than half—had put their names, not merely to a 'memorial', but to a Motion on the Order Paper asking for 'abolition or reduction'. No Minister or junior Minister—

not even, I think, a P.P.S.—however friendly in feeling, can put his name to such a Motion, and the Ministerial army numbers about 80, so the figure, 358, is extraordinary—and should have been effective, if 'the sovereign Parliament' means anything.

(*d*) The new Chancellor of the Exchequer, Mr Harold Macmillan, had a name for drive and independence, well earned by his housing achievements at the Ministry of Health. If anybody could stand up to the Treasury, it was thought, he might. Also, he had been a member of the famous publishing firm of Macmillan and Co. He must remember thankfully the failure of Sir Kingsley Wood's attempt to put a purchase tax on books (1940), and should have a fellow feeling for us.

Through the winter of 1955–6 the Press gave generous space to articles and letters: all the old, and many new, arguments were deployed. Two London evening papers[1] came out with leading articles in our favour (which is more, I think, than *The Times* or the *Daily Telegraph* has ever done). In public the wind set fair.

[2]

But danger threatened from a most inappropriate quarter. In January there began a long and astonishing correspondence between Mr Dingle Foot (for the Theatres Entertainment Tax Committee) and Sir William Emrys Williams, C.B.E., Secretary-General of the Arts Council of Great Britain, no less. The Arts Council was incorporated under Royal Charter on 9 August 1946 . . .

'. . . for the purpose of developing greater knowledge, understanding, and practice of the fine arts exclusively, and in particular to increase the accessibility of the fine arts to the public . . . to improve the standard of execution of the fine

[1] The *Evening Standard* and, I think, the *Evening News*.

arts and to advise and co-operate with Government Departments, Local Authorities and other bodies on any matters concerned directly or indirectly with those objects'.

It is financed by an annual grant from the Treasury. For the year 1954–5 the grant was £785,000: in 1956 £885,000—nearly half the amount taken by the Treasury, in Entertainments Tax, from the living theatre. It is for the Arts Council, said Mr H. Macmillan, on 12 June 1956, 'to divide this sum as it thinks best between Covent Garden and the many other organizations which it supports'.[1]

I am not one of those who yell 'Down with the British Council!' or decry the spending of public money on the Arts. On the contrary, I am glad that we are still civilized enough to stand by the sinking ship at Covent Garden, on exactly the same principle as I wish to see the turnover-tax taken off all other theatres. But when I read this shocking correspondence, I did feel that the Arts Council of Great Britain, as now administered, should not be allowed to spend one penny or control one person.

Mr Dingle Foot's first letter (26 January 1956) was provoked by some strange passages in the Arts Council's Annual Report for 1954-5.

'They seem to suggest,' he concluded, 'that all theatrical enterprise outside the special protection and patronage to be afforded by the Arts Council is unworthy of support or encouragement. This Committee would like to have an assurance that it is not the policy of the Arts Council to disparage the tax-paying as opposed to the tax-exempt and subsidized theatre or to approve of the constant closing of theatres to which the present difficulties of the former have led.'

[1] It is through the Arts Council that the Treasury subsidizes Covent Garden, and it is a convenient buffer when the State is accused of spending too much, or too little, or in the wrong quarters. The grant to Covent Garden in 1956 was £270,000—£20,000 more than the year before. 'Public funds' since the war, said the Chancellor, had provided £1,778,000 towards Covent Garden losses (*The Times*, 13 June 1956).

Sir William Williams replied at once:

'I should like to assure you, at the outset, that we have no desire whatever to disparage the work of the tax-paying theatres, with whose present difficulties we very much sympathize.'

But the disparaging note, the lofty note of disdain, keeps thrusting itself into Sir William's smooth and conciliatory argument. The 'commercial theatre', of course, is everywhere. Then 'The distinction must be drawn between art and entertainment'. (My hat! But how—and why?) 'The show business and the commercial theatre will solve this problem of housing (and everything else) on purely economic calculations.'—Then there was something about 'a further protective tariff for *serious* drama' and a reference to 'non-profit companies interested in art and not in business'.

As I ploughed through pages of this nauseating stuff I kept thinking of such gallant 'commercial' men of the theatre as Sir Nigel Playfair and Sir Charles Cochran, who faced the world without subsidies, who paid their own bills, and the tax as well, and so, according to the great Sir William Williams, were 'interested in business and not in art.'

All this might be dismissed as the idle insults of a highbrow insufficiently acquainted with the facts of life. But Mr Foot's relentless cross-examination revealed at last that these high thoughts were prompting low behaviour—by the Arts Council of Great Britain.

'It is our business here,' said Sir William, 'to give aid and comfort to the non-profit repertory theatres.'

Mr Foot replied:

'The Charter of the Arts Council imposes no such limitation on your scope of reference. On the contrary, it charges you with the general duty of encouraging the fine arts, including "their accessibility to the public throughout the

Realm". . . . Reports and figures submitted to this Committee show that the Entertainments Duty is prominent among the factors which are compelling so many theatres to close, and that, if the Duty was removed, a substantial number of these theatres would be able to stay open. This result is surely one which the Arts Council within its general mission might actively foster. Indeed, as the Arts Council is empowered to "co-operate" with "other bodies on any matters concerned directly or indirectly with its objects", it seems appropriate to invite your positive support of the objects of this Committee.'

Sir William then said that 'if we applied our share of public funds to the assistance of profit-distributing enterprises we should incur severe criticism in Parliament and elsewhere'. Mr Joseph Dean (for Mr Foot) replied that 'this committee is not inviting you to apply any part of your funds to the assistance of our campaign. This Committee is inviting the Arts Council to express its approval and support of our object, namely, the abolition of the Entertainments Duty on the living theatre'.

But even this was refused, for these strange reasons (I have put together some extracts from several letters):

'It is our business . . . to look after our own chicks which, in this case, are the non-profit repertory theatres. . . . Parliament has accepted the principle of protecting non-profit-distributing companies, and it is with these that the Arts Council is concerned. We are, in that sense, a vested interest. . . . If Entertainment Tax were cancelled, or even reduced, the non-profit companies would suffer financially. . . .' (How horribly 'commercial'! Reasons were given here to which I shall return.) 'We are conscious of the fact that, were the Tax to go, our own particular chicks would be in dire jeopardy. You may well think that these are inadequate reasons for our not joining in your campaign. But I hope that you will nevertheless appreciate that the reasons, for what they are worth, exist. The Arts Council has, from time to time, discussed the whole question and its members are of a divided mind on the principles involved. But they are entirely of one mind in seeing what the consequences would be to our own protégé's if the Tax were cancelled' (15 February).

In another letter (6 March), Sir William, warming to his work, wrote:

'If Entertainment Tax were cancelled *the immediate consequence would be the closure of many of the organizations we assist*, for we know that increased subsidies are at present out of the question. . . . Is it reasonable that we should associate ourselves with a campaign which would have *that unquestionable consequence*? Our only rational action is to remain neutral, which we are doing. We have made no public announcement whatever about Entertainment Tax and, to that extent, are at least not opposing your campaign. I do not see that more can be expected of us.'

In his final letter (12 March) Mr Joseph Dean wrote:

'I am sorry that the Arts Council should insist on dividing the theatre so absolutely into Tax-paying goats and State-subsidized sheep, with yourselves as shepherds of the latter. However, neutrality is better than hostility.' He added shrewdly: 'I hope that your policy of neutrality is not confined to making no public announcements but extends also to *any private consultations* you may have from time to time with the Treasury, or any other official body.'

THE GREAT INGRATITUDE

You may well wonder at Sir William's dire predictions of disaster to his 'chicks'. Why, after all, if Drury Lane is relieved of tax, should the Arts Theatre at Bath, or Bristol, which are not paying it, have to close at once as an 'unquestionable consequence'?

Let us go back to the letter of 15 February, and Sir

William's special 'reasons', which are even more surprising than his conclusions:

'If Entertainment Tax were cancelled, or even reduced, the non-profit companies would suffer financially. They would suffer on two counts. At present they pay royalty on nett receipts (i.e. after the deduction of tax-equivalent). This concession would go if the Tax went. At present, also, sharing terms (where they exist) are computed after the deduction of tax-equivalent. This, again, gives the non-profit companies a more favourable position than they would have if the tax were withdrawn.'

Anyone would suppose, from Sir William's words, that these 'concessions' were made by Parliament or the Treasury: so I must here explain their history and character—and remember that all these complications were caused by the innocent authors of the Zoo-Clause:

(*A*) *The Author*

In what is called the 'commercial' theatre the author draws a royalty of *x* per cent on the gross receipts LESS Entertainments Tax. This must have cost me thousands in my time: but it is a matter of custom and contract, and it shows that we agree with the managers when they say that the tax is really 'paid' by them—and not by the 'consumer.'

In the 'non-profit-distributing' theatre, where there is no tax, the author is entitled to draw royalty on the gross receipts without any deduction. But on 2 May 1947 the British League of Dramatists received a deputation from the Council of Repertory Theatres and, wishing to help the weak and struggling little companies, and not thinking it proper for their authors to 'cash-in' on a concession designed to help them, they agreed to approve the deduction of 'tax-equivalent' when the author's royalties were calculated. (An odd arrangement, you may think, for why should the author be the chief bearer of a tax where there is no tax? Why, for instance, should tax-equivalent not be deducted from the manager's salary?) But they made some stern conditions. It was to be made clear in every case that this was an 'act of grace' and that any author who insisted was entitled to draw his full royalty. The 'act of grace' intended for the weak and feeble has, of course, been abused. It is used by wealthy companies in London, and by some smaller people in the country. I have a manager friend who, quite innocently, thought that he was *compelled* by the Customs to deduct 'tax-equivalent' and has never consulted his authors at all. However, the League of British Dramatists still maintain their approval of these arrangements, so long as the tax endures: but their policy is the complete abolition of the tax.

(*B*) *The Manager*

Here is the manager's story, from one who 'wishes to remain anonymous':

'As a member of the Committee urging the abolition of the Entertainment Tax, I have become aware of the fact that the Arts Council has stated its intention to stand aloof, giving as one of its reasons the fact that such abolition might rob the non-profit distributing companies, which it supports, of some of their present advantages.

'I am very sad that such an attitude should have been adopted, especially so, in view of the fact that a year ago the Council of Repertory Theatres sent a resolution to the Chancellor of the Exchequer stating that though they were aware that abolition might place them at a disadvantage, nevertheless they thought that for the benefit of the theatre as a whole, the Tax should be abolished. It must be remembered that the Council of Repertory Theatres comprises amongst its members nearly all the drama companies subsidized by the Arts Council. I think that one of the elements that moved C.O.R.T. to pass this resolution was the knowledge that their present temporary advantages were fortuitous—that is to say they did not arise from, and were not inherent in, the Finance Act, but had come about as the result of private negotiations between interested parties.

'(1) Firstly there is the Landlord and Tenant agreement. It was the late Sir Reginald Rowe, then Treasurer of the Vic-Wells, who came to a gentleman's agreement with the Customs and drew up the standard rental agreement, which, with adaptation to circumstances, is used by all non-profit distributing companies. This ensured that the equivalent of the Tax should be paid intact to the producing companies, and the balance divided in agreed ratio between the theatre owners and the producing company. Up to 1939, when there were not more than three or four such companies touring or renting London theatres, this agreement was accepted without question by the theatre owners, who felt that the matter was too insignificant to warrant their concern.

The war, and the coming into being of certain influential non-profit-distributing companies, changed their attitude, and round about 1942 there was serious friction with the theatre owners. A ruling was sought from the Customs, and Lord Keynes arranged for Lewis Casson (then Drama Director of C.E.M.A.) to see the head of the Customs, who stated quite bluntly that the division of the takings was no concern of theirs. From their point of view once they had granted exemption, *the tax did not exist* and the contracting parties could make any division that they liked. It was, however, the late Stuart Cruikshank (father of the present Stuart) who decided that, as he was also a director of the most influential non-profit-distributing company, it would be wrong, *vis-à-vis* his competitors, for him to reap the benefit of a larger rental from the tax exemption. He laid it down that in all his future agreements, the sharing terms would be based only on the remaining sum after the equivalent of the tax had been deducted; and that this equivalent should be paid in full to the producing company. His example has been generally followed, but *it is not the law of the land*, and not all companies have adhered to it.

'(2) As regards the royalties, this question also did not

arise until the war because up till then most of the plays produced had been royalty-free. It was again the new influential non-profit-distributing companies in London who raised the problem in an acute form. At first they paid a percentage to actors and authors on the gross takings including the tax-equivalent. A violent press campaign was organized by their competitors, and again it was Lord Keynes who intervened in the summer of 1943. He first ordered the expulsion from C.E.M.A. of the company in question, but was mollified by the promise made that after the current contracts had expired, no future contracts would be made involving the payment of a royalty or percentage on the tax-equivalent. These incidents, however, had had their repercussions on the fortunes of the Repertory Theatres, who found themselves faced by varying demands. Sometimes the agents would accept a royalty on the nett, after the deduction of the equivalent. Other agents demanded a royalty on the gross takings including the equivalent. In 1946 C.O.R.T. came to a gentleman's agreement with the League of Dramatists whereby royalty should only be paid on the balance, after the deduction of the "equivalent". This agreement has been generally adhered to, though again it is not the law of the land. There have been exceptions. Until quite recently Somerset Maugham was rigid in his demand that non-profit-distributing companies should pay a higher royalty than those companies which had to pay the tax.

'You see, therefore, that these arrangements are flexible, and were the tax abolished it would not be beyond the wit of man to devise new agreements whereby the present advantages held by the non-profit-distributing companies could be maintained. Such an arrangement has, in fact, already taken place. In 1948 the Tax was cut by half. The Vic-Wells companies which, up till then, had been receiving 60 to 65 per cent of the nett takings, plus the equivalent of the tax, immediately demanded 65 to 70 per cent, and their demands were acceded to.'

So, in short, the authors and the managers had presented the non-profit companies with a nice knife with which to butter their bread and the Arts Council were using it to stab them in the back. Or, as I wrote to Hugh Gaitskell, the sergeant gives his water bottle to a wounded man: but when the sergeant tries to draw another the wounded man cries, 'Oy! You can't do that! That will put you on a level with ME!'

But how were poor Members of Parliament to know all this? All that they would hear would be, 'The Arts Council are against it.' I composed the following reply and sent it to a few of them:

ENTERTAINMENTS DUTY—LIVING THEATRE

'I learn that upon this subject a novel and astonishing argument has recently been circulated, with some effect, among Members of the House of Commons. The source is extraordinary; the argument—and the facts behind it—are erroneous; and it is necessary to expose and to refute them.

The Argument

(1) The argument is that the Entertainment Tax on the living theatre should be continued, since if it were abolished certain "non-profit" companies (producing "serious drama") would suffer financially, especially those in which the Arts Council are financially interested.

The Source

(2) The argument has been advanced by the Secretary General to the Arts Council, who writes, surprisingly, that "we here have a vested interest in one kind of theatre"—and therefore refuses even moral support to the others.

Objections

(3) The argument (apart from the detailed objections

which follow) rests upon a vicious principle—the maintenance of a tax upon the many in order to exempt the few.

(4) The argument, even if the principle were acceptable, does not stand up to examination in detail:

(*a*) The Council of Repertory Theatres, which might have been expected to support it, has voted, nine months ago, for the abolition of the Entertainment Tax.

(*b*) The Arts Council say—and this is their main contention—that "if Entertainment Tax were cancelled, or even reduced, the non-profit companies would suffer financially", for they would lose the benefit of certain "concessions" by the League of Dramatists, and, in some cases (where there are "sharing terms"), by the owners or managers of theatres. These are artificial but generous arrangements by which "tax-equivalent" is deducted from the gross takings where, in fact, no tax is paid, to the advantage of the non-profit companies and the detriment of authors and managers. (See Appendix 'C'.) These arrangements do not rest upon statute or Customs regulations; they are voluntary "acts of grace" which could be withdrawn tomorrow—and may well be. The contention, therefore, of the Arts Council is not only a classic example of ingratitude, but is quite invalid, and may soon be unavailable, as an argument for retaining the Entertainment Tax.

(*c*) The Arts Council say "If Entertainment Tax were cancelled the immediate consequence would be the closure of many of the organizations we assist". Whatever may be the plight of the Arts Council's own protégés, this would be, I am informed, a gross misstatement of the general position, and, as I have noted, is not supported by the Council of Repertory Theatres. In most cases, I am told, the disadvantages would in fact be small, and in proper cases could be remedied. Most of the companies are not on "sharing terms" so that the question of manager's "tax-equivalent" does not arise. They might lose, here and there, the automatic, and, in many cases, improper deduction of "tax-equivalent" from authors' royalties: but (A) there seems to be no strong reason why the author, the foundation of the whole affair, should be expected to subsidize "non-profit" companies, and (B) any author who in proper cases, e.g. an Arts Council company, was willing, could easily bestow the same benefit in other ways, as by accepting a reduced rate of royalty on gross takings.

(*d*) Under the Local Government Act, 1948, local authorities can, up to a 6*d*. rate, support local theatres, and this, I feel, would be a better way out than the extraction of bounty from authors and managers—and a suitable avenue for the activities of the Arts Council.

(5) (*a*) Apart from ingratitude, it is surely improper for the Arts Council, charged with the general duty of fostering the fine arts everywhere, to refuse, for the sake of its "vested interest" in certain small non-profit companies, to give even moral support to the main body of the British Theatre, which is fighting a difficult battle with foreign competitors in London and other big cities. What would be said if we proposed that British, but not American, plays should be exempt from tax?

(*b*) Ordinary theatre folk resent and reject the distinction made between the "commercial" and the "artistic" or "serious" drama. All good entertainment, as a High Court Judge said on the Bench the other day, is artistic.

(*c*) But then it is said, by Mr Levy and his school of thought: "Those who do not like paying the tax can go 'non-profit'." This again, if it were true, would be to introduce a novel and dangerous principle, not likely to be proposed or accepted in the newspaper or book trade. (I have, by the way, a private suspicion that the Arts Council are interested not only in art but power, and would like to see everyone driven by punitive taxation into their domain.)[1] But it is not correct. The non-profit arrangements involve a form of censorship. "Customs and Excise," says the Secretary of the Arts Council, "keep a watch on the non-profit-distributing companies (which are exempt from tax) to see that they do not go in for the more lucrative forms of light entertainment, and that they stick to the more perilous field of 'serious' repertory." "Music hall or other variety entertainments" are excluded by Customs regulations (Notice 100), which also says "in considering whether the aims, etc., of a society are partly educational . . . exemption may be allowable for an *occasional* light work". In other words, it would be quite impossible for a new Cochran, a new Novello or Coward, or a new Gilbert and Sullivan to produce a series of expensive musical plays, however "artistic", under the non-profit banner. Nor, I may add, is sufficient capital likely to be forthcoming in that fiercely competitive field under the limitations laid down by the non-profit regulations.

(*d*) Naturally, we all share the desire of the Arts Council that the little theatres should survive, however humbly, throughout the country. But there are "good", deserving, but struggling efforts in the big theatres of London and other cities too. In our anxiety to assist the weaklings let us not forget the main fighting forces. I wrote 14 or 15 pieces for those "commercial" fellows Sir Nigel Playfair and Sir Charles Cochran. All, I think, were as "artistic" as anything the Arts Council has given us. All were damaged by the tax, and some destroyed. Few, because of the tax, showed a profit.

[1] Sir Irving Albery, I see, in 1943, when criticizing the 'non-profit abuses', said prophetically: 'If the matter is allowed to go too far along present lines we shall get an amateur dictatorship running the drama of the country, and that is most undesirable.'

The present generation of managers is not highly thought of in some quarters. Perhaps, if they were relieved of this burden, and given a fairer fight, new Playfairs and Cochrans would appear among them. (I think I can see one or two on the horizon already.) But not one of the Arts Council's "serious" little companies is likely to recapture Drury Lane.

(6) The argument fails, therefore, in equity, fact, and reason, and I am sure you will dismiss it from your mind.'

But we were far from sure.

The weary drill of every year was done once more, the anxious conferences, the careful drafting (I wonder sometimes what the total bill can be for all the time and trouble of busy leaders thus distracted from their proper work). The usual deputation of managers attended at the Treasury and was kindly received by the Financial Secretary, Mr Brooke.

Another deputation, including some actors, and one humble author, attended a meeting of private Members at the House of Commons—Sir Tom O'Brien in the chair. Many Members sat patiently and listened attentively for an hour and a half—a very hopeful sign, for at that time of day, as I know, Members have many calls upon them, and those upstairs meetings can be ineffective or dangerous.

But behind all the hopes lurked the thought of the Arts Council of Great Britain, a body close to the Treasury—and 'neutral'. The Treasury, we knew, like to be 'neutral' too.

SAD INTERLUDE—*THE WATER GIPSIES*

On 24 March 1956—Boat Race Day—Mr Peter Saunders was reluctantly compelled to end the run of *The Water Gipsies*, by Vivian Ellis and myself, at The Winter Garden Theatre, after a run of only 7½ months. The story, though there are hundreds like it, is a good illustration of our general theme. The plan, and confident hope, had been to keep running through the summer and into the winter. But Fate decided—as it had decided twice before in my modest theatrical career—that our leading lady, the brilliant Dora Bryan, was to have a baby and must leave the company. This is one of the natural hazards of the theatre, which we accept as cheerfully as we can: but an enterprise subject to such unpredictable and unavoidable calamities ought not to suffer a turnover tax. But for the tax we could still, I believe, have carried on. I gave the figures, so far as I know them, in a letter to the *Daily Telegraph:*

'Sir,—In the last week (as in the first) of its London run the public paid £3,700 to see the British musical play, *The Water Gipsies*—and the State took £600 out of the till. For 30 weeks the Treasury has been extracting an average of £500 a week, or £15,000 in all. The cost of production, I am told, was £28,000. The weekly receipts have amply covered the high weekly costs of a musical show, and if he had been allowed to keep that £15,000 the manager, in spite of other troubles, would have been able to carry on and make a profit in the end. As it is, although a quarter of a million people have seen and enjoyed his brave production, the result for him is, I believe, a loss. But the State, which has risked nothing and contributed nothing, has £15,000.

'I will not repeat all the arguments against this odd arrangement. But I wish we could be told what, in the Treasury view, is the purpose and merit of this tax:

(*a*) Does it help the export drive?
(*b*) Does it "mop up inflationary pressure"?
(*c*) Is it intended to reduce consumption?
(*d*) Is it to keep out undesirable imports—and which?
(*e*) Is it simply a revenue tax?

'If the last is right, it would be interesting to know what it costs to collect that miserable two million pounds (from the living theatre), and what is lost, in a case like this, by way of income tax, profit tax, purchase tax, etc., to say nothing of unemployment pay.'

After the announcement that the play was coming off the people flocked to the theatre again. On the last, tumultuous but melancholy night, Peter Saunders induced me to make a speech from our box. I said, among other things, that I would do no more in the fight for the British 'musical' till the Entertainments Tax was taken off. And I meant it. So, for all I know, 1956 has seen my last appearance in the theatre.

To complete the sad story—not long after the play was taken off, poor Dora Bryan lost her baby.

[3]

On 17 April Mr Harold Macmillan 'opened' his first Budget. The Entertainments Duty was not mentioned—not a word of apology or regret to the 358 Members. But the Finance Bill was still to come. I wrote, among other things, to the patient *Times*:

'There is a constitutional point of high importance. More than half the House of Commons (about 350 members) have put their names to a motion demanding the abolition or reduction of the theatre tax. The Civil Servants of the Treasury have brushed them aside as if they were so many flies. But are they? The House of Lords is out, I know; but has the House of Commons no control of Finance? Does "Grievances before Supply" mean nothing now? I hope the private Members will not take this insult lying down. . . . I hope that the 350 Members will stand up to the Treasury as we stood up to Sir Kingsley Wood in 1940 when we made him withdraw his purchase tax on newspapers and books. Then, with Hitler at the door, we said: "No tax upon the things of the mind"—and we prevailed. The 350 Members have only to make it clear that they will vote for their motion at whatever cost, and they will have their way.

At the worst, it would be a fine advertisement for the British Parliament if a Government fell on such a point of principle. For one of the high tests of any country is its treatment of the arts and, yes, the "entertainments", without which we might as well be pigs in "full employment".'

In the general Budget debate, Mr Henry Brooke said that to reduce this Duty would be 'out of tune with the theme and purpose of the Budget'.

In their final speeches for the Opposition—and this disturbed me more than Mr Brooke's recitations from the Treasury Anthology—neither Mr Douglas Jay nor Dr Dalton mentioned the subject. True, they had many much bigger things to discuss: but this one (abolition) had appeared in their Election Manifesto, and, as a rule, a fighting Opposition, on the Budget, takes a hammer to every nail in sight. I sniffed the air and I said: 'Benn Levy?' I had no kind of evidence. All the winter we had been airing our case in articles and letters, and many correspondents, as usual, had dug up some of the old dead objections, 'Will prices be reduced?'—'Good plays always prosper', etc. There had not been a word from the historic enemy, Benn Levy. It was pure intuition—impure suspicion—call it what you will—but I sniffed the air and said to myself, with respectful awe, 'Benn Levy?'

[4]

After the Budget there was a very full meeting of the Theatres Entertainment Tax Committee which, though I am not a member, Mr Dingle Foot invited me to attend. It impressed, but saddened me. I often think that the theatre's worst enemy is the man who wrote that brave but silly song, 'There's No Business Like Show Business'—to which the right answer is 'Thank God!' or 'Can you wonder?'—for no other 'business' in the world would even try to live under similar conditions. This meeting was not 'Show Business', as the people have been taught to imagine it. Here was no gathering of hard-faced rapacious 'business' or 'bricks and mortar' men. There was, for example, an eager lady from the British Drama League, which none could call a 'commercial' body. There was an actor, and a high representative of Actors' Equity. There was a musician: and very often, I believe, the League of Dramatists send an 'observer'. There was Sir Tom O'Brien, the strong but sunny Labour Member, secretary to the Theatre and Kine Employees' Trade Union. There were managers too, some of the men who choose the plays and risk their money—Mr S. E. (Bill) Linnit, Chairman of the Theatres' National Committee, and President of the Society of West End Theatre Managers (who then had running the successful *Salad Days* and, less successful, a charming but expensive British musical, *A Girl Called Jo*)[1]—Mr Frederic Carter of Associated Theatres, who had just put on a new play by Noel Coward and, because of the Budget, had raised his prices—Mr Prince Littler, who gave me the astonishing figures of a 'successful' year at Drury Lane[2]—Mr Jack de Leon, who, all his life, has been bravely producing, win or lose, what he thought was 'good'—my humble self who no longer had any personal interest in the affair—and many others. There were no men there, perhaps, with such creative records, such glowing names, as Nigel Playfair and Charles Cochran at the end of their careers. But these men are younger; and their costs are twice or thrice what Cochran's were. High bills and taxes may tempt or drive them, here and there, to take the line of least resistance. But give them a fairer fight, and

[1] Alas, in August 1956, 'Bill' Linnit died, aged 58, a sudden and severe loss to the theatre and his countless friends. He was a man of charm, taste, dignity, and judgment, a leader—and a producer—who will be genuinely missed. He was always keen and active in this particular cause, and the last word I had from him, just before his death, was a kind and helpful letter about this little book. In it he recalled the points he had made, briefly but effectively, at the House of Commons meeting. It was, I think, his last public speech. Many will remember him long.

[2] See Appendix 'A'.

some great names may grow among them still. At all events, here were earnest men, believing in the virtue of their work and the justice of their cause, and no more deserving to be dubbed 'commercial' than that famous firm of publishers, Macmillan and Co.

They had been summoned to discuss (*a*) plans of action for the Committee stage of the Finance Bill, and (*b*) the alarming correspondence with the Arts Council. On (*a*) someone said confidently, 'Anyhow, the Labour Party's on our side'. I said, I remember, 'Are you quite sure? I have a feeling Benn Levy's been up to something.' On (*b*) someone revealed that Mr Benn Levy was the chairman of the Drama Panel of the Arts Council, which I did not know.

The Committee took the gravest view of the attitude of the Arts Council. Until that was changed, said one or two, our cause was hopeless. It was decided to propose a meeting between a few members of the Committee and Sir William Williams.[1]

We parted, that day, in a grim despondent mood, and I felt very sorry for everyone. This year, after forty years, success, we had thought, was in sight at last. The Chancellor himself had not said a word and, with all-party pressure, might be persuaded to relent. We had faced and defeated all our old and open enemies—but here was a new and secret foe, not one who aired his opinions in public, as we did, and could be knocked on the head, but a hidden enemy behind the throne. The Arts Council had the ear of the Treasury and could whisper into it every day the ludicrous, treacherous, but seductive advice: 'Please go on taxing the theatre for the theatre's good.' And one of its members, I suspected, might have muttered the same thing to our best ally, the Labour Party. This, however, was only my own surmise, and, after all, Sir William had promised that he was 'neutral'. We *knew* nothing.

[1] This invitation, after many days, was declined—'no useful purpose—no more to be said', etc.

HAPPY ACCIDENT

Accident, pure accident, then took a hand, as it often does in political affairs. (I never know what to think about this. The impact of accident makes the story more 'dramatic': but if the right result is reached through accident only, is this a good mark for 'democracy'?) By accident, I was invited again to the Royal Academy Dinner (this does not happen every year). By accident, at the bottom of the great staircase, I met my fellow Wykehamist, Mr Hugh Gaitskell, Leader of the Opposition, and we walked up together. At the top, just before we separated, I said to myself, 'This is a dirty trick. This poor fellow is having a worrying time' (it was not long after the Kruschev dinner) 'and tonight he's having a night off. I should leave him alone. But,' I added to myself, 'it's an opportunity I must not miss.' So I said, 'By the way, are your people all right about the Entertainment Tax?'

Mr Gaitskell said, 'Yes.—But,' he went on, with an air of surprise, 'there seems to be some opposition.'

'Benn Levy?' I said, pricking up my long sagacious ears.

'Yes,' said Mr G. 'He's sent in a long memorandum. But nowadays I pass on all those things to Harold Wilson.'

'I thought as much,' I said. 'Thank you.' And we parted.

So my unworthy intuitions were correct. My old friend Benn had been secretly 'up to something'. But we still had no notion (*a*) what he had written to Mr Gaitskell, and (*b*) whether he had written in the same terms to the Treasury. If I have a bright idea which I wish to press upon Ministers or Members I blurt the whole thing out in *The Times* or elsewhere. Then anybody can knock it about, and if the affair comes up in Parliament everyone knows what he has to answer. It is democratic—but dangerous. It is much cleverer, clearly—and I must remember this in future—to write private memoranda to those in power. For now the theatre did not know what it had to answer. Mr. Levy, I guessed (correctly), would have written whatever he did write 'in his private capacity': but the fact that he was Chairman of the Drama Panel of the Arts Council, and a member of the Executive Committee of the League of Dramatists, was quite likely to leak out and impress the uninformed, the new Member, for example, who did not know all that we did.

But, to be fair, I do not know what else, in his position, Mr Levy could have done. The Arts Council was 'neutral': the League of Dramatists was for abolition. He could hardly have expressed his opinions in public. He might, of course, have kept quiet. But he is like me, poor man: he has to keep on.

So, the next day, I wrote to Mr. Gaitskell about our little talk. I asked him (but without much hope) whether he could possibly let me see a copy of the Levy memorandum as the theatre folk were anxious to know 'what they had to answer'. Meanwhile, I assumed that Benn had said the sort of thing the Arts Council had said, and I gave the answers to it (see page 124). Mr Gaitskell replied in cordial terms and said that he had passed me on to Mr Harold Wilson. Faint but pursuing, I wrote to Mr Wilson, developing and explaining a point or two. I was told later that these two letters had come 'most opportunely' for the Levy poison had worked strongly, and one important Group (of the Parliamentary Labour Party) had already decided to support the Levy policy. The Finance Committee, though, fortified by my information, took the other view. There were joint meetings, etc., and eventually—but I go too fast. Anyway, Say not the struggle naught availeth. . . .

Every event and deed, of course, was reported at once to Dingle Foot, the campaign leader, and 'Bill' Linnit, the leader of the managers. They were still eager to see the Levy Memorandum. There were some signs of the poison having reached the Conservative ranks—Members who had been heard to say, 'Oh, I understand it all now. If they don't want to pay the tax they needn't'. Dingle Foot asked me if I would try to get a copy from Benn Levy himself, and I did

—that is, I tried. Not wishing to drag Mr Gaitskell in, I began 'A little bird told me . . .'

Benn replied merrily:

'You and your little bird! As far as my own views are concerned you must know already what you have to answer, for I assure you they haven't changed with the years. I thought and said that halving the Tax was a mistake and that to abolish it would be another. My reasons have been given in extenso and ad nauseam in Parliament, in the Press, in meetings, and in controversy with yourself.

'If you have not been able to answer them throughout the years, I don't see why you should be able to now!

'Nevertheless, despite your indefatigable addiction to bad causes, I love you still.'

I wish I could understand the mind of this good man. 'A mistake' to reduce the turnover tax on the theatre from 30 per cent to about 15 per cent (that was his leader, Sir Stafford Cripps). And this is a dramatist who has had plays produced by 'commercial' managers in London, and hopes, I imagine, to have more.

He did not, in his letter, admit that he had sent any document to anybody, nor did he even mention my polite request for a copy. But on the telephone he did say that he had been 'consulted' by some members of his Party, and had naturally obliged. He said that certainly he would not send me a copy of a 'private communication'. Would I? (To this there were a good many answers which I did not utter.) I mentioned the correspondence with the Arts Council and its promise of 'neutrality'. He said, as I expected, that he was entitled to write anything 'in his private capacity': but he added that the Drama Panel had not considered the matter at all (which makes Sir William Williams' letters more extraordinary still). Benn said too that he was sick of the subject and was not going to be 'drawn into controversy'. Considering how large a cat he had loosed among the pigeons, I laughed heartily at that.

THE DRAMATISTS

Meanwhile—so many are the watertight compartments of life—the League of Dramatists knew nothing about the Arts Council correspondence. I informed Miss M. E. Barber, the secretary, of the way in which their 'acts of grace' were being abused; and on 15 May I was invited to attend at a meeting of the Executive Committee. Mr Peter Ustinov was in the chair. I was given a seat next to Benn Levy, and was asked to develop the views I had expressed in writing.

At the risk of doing the wrong thing, I must record one episode which is like the famous occasion when 'the dog did not bark in the night'. At one moment I said, as one dramatist to another, 'By the way, Benn, did you write to the Treasury too?' My old colleague looked down his nose for some seconds and then said: 'You're here to answer questions, Alan, not to ask them.' 'Very well,' I said.

Mr Peter Ustinov is as hot for abolition as I am. When I withdrew, I am told, there was a long and 'animated' discussion, and it was, I believe, decided to send a protesting letter to the Arts Council.

[5]

But we still did not know exactly what had been written —indeed, we do not know to this day. Mr Dingle Foot and his men considered many plans to prevent the detachment of any of their 358 signatories from the true faith. A memorandum was sent to them all, and the various 'unions' represented on the Committee were asked to write as well. The British Drama League wrote to their 6,000 members all over the country. What a life!

One small shrewd move pleased me. I had told the chiefs of staff about Benn Levy's remark that the Drama Panel of the Arts Council 'had not considered the matter at all'. It was decided to send copies of the famous 'correspondence' to every member of the Drama Panel. They might, it was thought, care to know what the Council was up to in the field of drama.

Here is the excellent Memorandum:

(*a*) THE THEATRE CASE

Memorandum in Support of New Clauses to the Finance (No. 2) Bill, 1956, Seeking to Abolish the Entertainments Duty on the Living Theatre

The case in favour of the abolition of the tax on the Living Theatre may be summarized as follows:

Present Situation

In the last two or three years a new situation of extreme urgency has developed and is continuing to worsen. The position in the provinces is particularly serious. A list of more than 80 provincial theatres which in recent years have been forced to close down is set out in the attached Appendix. Some two dozen of these theatres were closed or converted during last year (1955).

Even where theatres have managed to survive, the stringent financial conditions under which they operate are compelling them to present fewer plays with fewer sets, smaller casts, and extremely small or no orchestras. Hence it is not surprising that the number of entertainments touring the provincial theatres has been steadily falling over the past few years. For instance, the number of shows on tour in October 1955 was only 75 as compared with 98 in October 1953, and 110 in October 1951.

Following the intensive competition from the cinema which began earlier in the century the living theatre is now faced with the additional competition caused by the spread of television throughout the country. The number of television licences has already increased from under 345,000 in 1950 to over 5,000,000 in 1955, and an additional factor is the opening of the Independent Television Service in September last year.

The living theatre finds particular difficulty in meeting this new competition for several reasons. It cannot increase its output because the number of its weekly performances is necessarily limited and it is not allowed to open on Sundays. The theatre cannot increase the number of its seats and experience has proved that it can only to a very limited and inadequate extent pass on its increased costs to the consumer by way of increased seat prices.

The Consequences of the Decline of the Theatre

All the factors contributing to the present decline in the theatrical world are likely to continue and indeed to become more acute. The only factor which can produce a change for the better, namely the abolition of the Entertainments Duty, is in the hands of the Chancellor. Unless that relief is given the probability is that the living theatre will disappear over a large part of the country and will only survive to a limited extent in the West End of London. This would be an irreparable loss to our national life, and it would also have a most damaging effect on the maintenance of quality so far as the production of films, sound broadcasts, and television are concerned in that all of them depend on a continuous and ample supply of trained actors, variety artistes, and other stage performers, who can only learn their job properly in the living theatre.

Nor must it be overlooked that there is already a far higher percentage of unemployment among actors and actresses than the rest of the community (approximately 13 per cent as opposed to 1 per cent). Once these experienced artists are lost to the theatre it will not be easy to replace them.

The Effect of the Entertainments Duty on the Theatre Industry

Although admittedly the Entertainments Duty is not the only main cause of the decline of the living theatre it does under present conditions assume a much greater relative importance than ever before. It has to be paid whether or not productions run at a profit and amounting as it does to a levy on turnover averaging about 14 per cent it often makes the whole difference between success and failure. *It has been estimated that the cost of production of a play today is three times the pre-war figure and five times for a musical show.* The running costs of both are about threefold. The result is that any loss is correspondingly greater, the period over which initial costs can be recovered is longer and unless a play proves an immediate and continued success the manager is often forced to cut his losses and withdraw it before it has had a fair chance of winning public approval. Moreover, the loss when it occurs is virtually a total loss because the physical assets of a play which has failed have no appreciable market value.

There is ample evidence to show that the decisive cause why many theatres have gone out of business has been the Entertainments Duty. An analysis made of returns by provincial theatres for the year 1954 and the first six months of 1955 shows losses on individual theatres ranging up to a maximum of £16,148 and in almost every case this loss would have been covered by the amount of Duty paid. The following examples are taken from widely scattered towns throughout the country:

		Year 1954		*Half-year to 30.6.55*	
Theatre	*Situation*	*Duty paid*	*Loss suffered*	*Duty paid*	*Loss suffered*
		£	£	£	£
A	Northern Industrial Town	13,083	2,949	6,914	2,670
B	Midland Town	9,393	1,763	4,811	1,779
C	Home Counties Town	16,562	(3,986) profit	6,890	2,071
D	Southern Counties Town (2 theatres)	17,231	4,962	7,084	6,240
E	Large Scottish Town	17,127	9,005	6,844	4,475
F	Large Welsh Town	7,297	4,255	4,164	2,445
G	London Suburb	12,543	663	5,781	2,466
H	London Suburb	11,048	9,213	4,434	4,319
I	London Suburb	5,190	6,948	2,365	5,333

It should be pointed out that considerable invested capital was involved in each of the above-mentioned cases, upon which neither interest nor dividend could be paid.

Although there is a general impression that conditions for theatres in the West End of London are much more favourable, an analysis shows that during recent years a very large percentage failed even to recover their production costs. This is borne out by the following table:

	Number of new Productions	*Number known to have recovered Production Costs*	*Number unsuccessful*	*Percentage of failures*
1952-3	64	25	39	60·94
1953-4	70	25	45	64·29
1955	54	9	45	83·3

It should also be made clear that, if the Duty is abolished, the whole amount will not accrue to the funds of the theatre, but will be divided between the theatre and the production companies, thereby assisting the theatre to survive with no more than a modest profit and encouraging the production companies to present a wider range and higher class of entertainment.

Anomalies of the Entertainments Duty

During recent years a number of anomalies have grown up with regard to the application of the Entertainments Duty on the living theatre and these can only be satisfactorily disposed of by its total abolition. Some of the more outstanding anomalies are the following:

(1) Companies whose aims are partly educational and who do not distribute their profits are exempted not only from the Entertainments Duty but also in some cases from Income Tax. Thus in Bristol at Christmas this year whilst the Theatre Royal could stage a tax-free Christmas play, the Hippodrome, presenting

pantomime, had to hand over approximately 14 per cent of their hard-won box office revenue in the form of Entertainments Duty (see Note below).

(2) The music-hall, an intrinsic part of British theatrical tradition, is excluded by Statute from the above tax-exempt provisions.

(3) Whilst all music-halls and revues are obliged to pay Entertainments Duty, similar performances in the form of cabarets in hotels, restaurants, and clubs are immune.[1]

(4) Entertainments given to not more than 400 people in a place with a population of less than 2,000 are exempt as are also amateur theatrical performances given under certain conditions.

(5) Whilst, subject to the above exemptions, the State taxes theatres generally throughout the land, it subsidizes a small selected number through the Arts Council, which in the year ending 31 March 1955 spent over £550,000 on subsidizing music and drama. Also under the Local Government Act 1948 local authorities may subsidize any theatre to the extent of the product of a sixpenny rate.

(6) Whilst theatres are in desperate competition with television, the State is subsidizing commercial television to the extent of £750,000 per annum for a period of ten years together with initial capital advances up to £2,000,000.

Note. It has recently been suggested that some non-profit-distributing repertory companies might suffer financially by the total abolition of the Entertainments Duty on the living theatre. It is, of course, true that they would lose their privileged position, and might have to pay a few pounds by way of authors' royalties, in so far as this would be based on gross takings (including the abolished tax) instead of on

[1] But not in the United States. The Federal tax on 'admissions' to 'cabarets, roof-gardens, etc.', yields $47,000,000 (1953).

the net receipts (excluding the exemption) as at present.

Apart from this, such companies would not be affected financially by abolition unless they were on a sharing basis with the management of the theatre where they were playing. In such cases, however, with the Entertainments Tax abolished, the sharing percentage would in all probability be increased to leave the touring producer in much the same position as today.

In any event the Council of Repertory Theatres recently passed a resolution in favour of the complete abolition of the Entertainments Duty on the living theatre, and they still maintain that point of view, since they appreciate that repertory theatres as a whole would benefit from the all-round improvement in theatre conditions which would result from abolition of the tax.

Revenue from Entertainments Duty

The revenue from Entertainments Duty on the living theatre for the year ended 31 March 1956 amounted to £2 million as against £2·17 million in the previous financial year, and £2·4 million in the year before. The net cost of the complete abolition of the Duty would, however, be substantially less. It would be offset not only by increased Income Tax revenue resulting from greater solvency but also by a decreased drain on the National Insurance funds. (At present over 2,000 people normally employed on the stage are drawing unemployment benefit weekly.) The ultimate loss to the revenue of abolishing the Entertainments Duty on the living theatre would probably be less than £1 million per annum and the sacrifice of such an amount would surely be a very small price to pay for the survival of the theatre.

It is suggested that the abolition of the Entertainments Duty on the living theatre would necessitate a similar concession with regard to cinematograph performances; it must not be forgotten that the circumstances of the two are quite different. This has already been recognized by the

Government in the two different scales of Duty. Again, as will be seen from the Appendix, several theatres which have closed have been re-opened as cinemas because, despite the higher scale of Duty applying to cinematograph entertainments, these places can still be operated more economically as cinemas than as live theatres.

Entertainments Duty and Parliament

There is strong and widespread support amongst all Parties in Parliament for the abolition of the Entertainments Duty on the living theatre. A Motion was recently placed on the Order Paper of the House of Commons, signed by 358 Members of all Parties, in the following terms:

'THE LIVING THEATRE: That this House, realizing the importance to the prestige, culture and well-being of the nation of preserving the living theatre, and noting with concern the continual closing of theatres and music-halls in all parts of the country resulting mainly from losses caused by box office receipts less entertainments duty falling below minimum running costs, urges Her Majesty's Government to investigate the situation without delay, and, in particular, to consider to what extent further closings can be avoided by extending the present limited range of exemptions from entertainments duty to include all forms of entertainment in which the performers are personally present and performing.'

Again, at the Trades Union Congress in 1954 a resolution in the following terms was unanimously passed:

'This Annual Congress expresses grave concern at the high level of unemployment in the entertainment industry and professions. It declares that the development of the arts and entertainment is essential for the general well-being of the people and the preservation of our own national culture. It therefore calls for much greater financial assistance to cultural and entertainment activities of all kinds by both the Government and local authorities and in particular for:

(i) the abolition of the Entertainments Duty on the live theatre;
(ii) remission of duty for cinemas employing live entertainment;
(iii) encouragement of local authorities to make full use of their powers under the Local Government Act to promote and maintain local culture and entertainment.'

Finally, in the official policy statement of the Labour Party, published before the Election in 1955, a declaration was made that it was part of the Party's policy to 'abolish the tax on sport and the living theatre'.

Conclusion

Both last year and this year we have been at the greatest pains in no way to exaggerate our case or to make any statement which could not be fully substantiated. We have never suggested that the Entertainments Duty is the sole, or even the principal, cause of the difficulties with which the living theatre is now confronted. Our contention is that, in the circumstances which now prevail, the relative importance of the Duty is greater than ever before. It was always, as we maintain and as is generally conceded, an unjust imposition. Now the point has been reached at which the survival of the living theatre over a great part of this country quite literally depends upon whether or not the Duty is abolished. The loss of revenue resulting from its abolition would be very small. The loss in every other respect resulting from its continuance will be immense and may well be irreparable.

The Chancellor's Present View

Referring to the various claims for concessions on Entertainments Duty the Financial Secretary to the Treasury stated during the debate on the Budget proposals (19 April 1956), that the Chancellor had given consideration to the matter but had come to the conclusion 'that the case for making any changes in the duty was not so strong that he ought to propose any change in his Budget this year, when a change of that sort would have been quite out of tune with the whole purpose and theme of his Budget.' He went on to say that 'In saying that he cannot see his way to doing anything in that respect this year, my right hon. Friend is not saying that nothing will be done as long as he is Chancellor' . . . but ' to come forward with proposals for making concessions in Entertainments Duty here and now would be strange indeed in a Budget the main purpose and object of which is to encourage people to save and not to spend.'

In so far as the main purpose of the Budget was related to the avoidance of inflation and the increasing of exports it is not clear that the remission of a tax on the living Theatre bringing in only £2 million a year has any very obvious relation to this purpose, nor would the abolition of this tax have any important bearing on saving or spending. In other words, whilst the abolition of the tax on the living theatre may be irrelevant to the main 'theme' of this year's Budget it would in no way disturb it.

But the survival of the living theatre is of vital importance to the culture and well-being of the country, and theatrical enterprise cannot be turned off or on like a tap. If our theatres are allowed to perish during this period of financial stringency it will not be possible to revive them when better times are with us, *and the country will have suffered an irreparable loss without any compensating advantage whatsoever.*

Here followed a lamentable list of 93 theatres which have closed, or been converted to other purposes, in recent years.

I should like to add to that some unofficial reflections of my own (from the *Evening Standard*) on

THE RIVALS

Or, Sunday On The Air

In 1916 the cinema was a child; the 'talking pictures' were a dream; the B.B.C. was not imagined—much less television and the I.T.A. (and the cinema, like the theatre, was closed on Sunday). Since then, a revolution has taken place in the entertainment world: but the Act of 1916 remains. When these great new rivals grew to manhood the State should have said: 'We will scrap the Act of 1916, survey the whole field of "entertainment"—and start again' —that is, if it still insisted on taxing thought, beauty, and fun. The theatre is not simply an out-of-date institution complaining of 'redundancy': it complains—and this is not generally realized—that, in relation to its modern rivals, it is unfairly treated by the law.[1]

It is the Lord's Day: and the nobler citizens gratefully reflect that today the wicked playhouses will have to close their doors. For by the Sunday Observance Act, 1781: 'If a house, room, or place be opened for any public entertainment, or for debating upon any subject, on Sunday, to which persons are admitted only by payment, the keepers thereof shall forfeit £200.' So by the wise prevision of George III and his Parliament, the citizen is protected from the painted 'mummer' and his baleful influence, and the painted mummers are free of worldly labour.

But George III and his Ministers never imagined Marconi. From 8.0 in the morning till midnight the B.B.C. is humming with 'worldly labour.' On Sunday, 22 January

[1] And not only by the law. The newspapers print, for nothing, all the radio and racing programmes—not to mention news paragraphs on the night that Princess Margaret is to attend 'What's My Line?', etc., on television. But they charge the theatres heavily for inserting their modest announcements of time, place, and play. These may cost a single theatre as much as £100 a week. In the national paper with the greatest circulation there can, for economic reasons, be no theatrical advertisements at all. The newspapers, I am sure, have a good answer, but I do not know what it is.

1956, the B.B.C. gave us twenty musical entertainments, ranging from a Russian opera and a symphony concert to briefer dance-bands and gramophone recitals. But what would have upset George III would have been the prevalence of the wicked playhouse. I marked, I see, 10 items S for Stage. Most of the radio items, it is true, were 'recordings'—that is, the wretched mummers were not in fact doing any worldly labour that day. Still, there were 60 or 70 of them exercising their baleful influence in the homes of the people: and earning money for it. And what would George III have thought of the television programme? A sort of variety show, a play for children, performed by 13 mummers; a play for grown-ups, blatantly advertised as 'Sunday Night Theatre' (14 mummers), and a 'special performance' of a circus. I make the total about forty mummers, all hard at it on the Lord's Day, and thrusting their painted faces into the home.

I.T.V. would shock George III even more. For here the big boast is 'Sunday Night Music Hall' at 8.0. After that, at 9.0, comes 'Theatre Royal', and at 9.30 'America's No. 1 comedy programme'. Earlier, at 3.0, there was 'Movie Magazine', and at 3.30 'Stage One'—'Your Anglo-American Theatre . . .'—live mummers in all.

At 4.0 p.m. the cinemas opened their doors, and at 4.30 the first moving pictures were shown. But the cinemas, unlike the B.B.C. or I.T.V., pay a heavy Entertainment Tax (up to 80 per cent on the original price of the seats), and are compelled by law to give a proportion of their Sunday takings to charity. This is the most luminous piece of humbug on the Statute Book.

O, Edison! O, Signor Marconi! O, Mr Baird! What have you made of the famous British Sunday? I do not wish to interfere with the people's fun. But I should like to say a kind word for the wicked playhouse. The theatre can have no share in this orgy of sabbatical entertainment, though its mummer sons and daughters, whether screened, recorded, or present in person, may earn money on that day by the arts that she has taught them and the names that she has assisted them to make. She may well feel wounded, especially if the same sons and daughters piously declare that they are against Sunday opening and must 'have their Sunday free'. . . . The mummers, I believe, are still divided on the point, and, even if they were not, the State is most unlikely to change the law. But the State might well consider the new Sunday situation, when Mother Theatre raises her despairing plea against the Entertainment Tax. All her great rivals can operate seven days a week—she for six only. The cinema pays Entertainment Tax, and at a much higher rate. But it still draws all the Sunday money.

The average theatre can give eight performances a week, not more than 24 hours in all: and pays a purchase tax of, roughly, 3*s*. in the £ on every ticket. A radio licence (without television) costs £1, but gives the subscriber 120 hours of entertainment in the week, or 6,240 hours in a year. From that £1 the Treasury snatches 1*s*. 10*d*. only. Last year it took £2,000,000 from the impregnable B.B.C. and £2,400,000 from the precarious theatre. Roughly, the wicked playhouse bears a tax of 1*s*. in the £ on every hour of its limited 24: while the radio subscriber gets 26 hours of entertainment for 1*d*., of which the Treasury takes one-tenth of a penny or less. The television subscriber, I reckon, gets 5 hours of entertainment for 1*d*.: on Sunday he gets 8 hours. (Yes, yes, I know, he has to buy his set, etc.: but that is not the point.)

Again, the theatre—and the cinema—have to lure the citizens through fog, snow, rain, frost or heat-wave, traffic-jams, and parking troubles, and compete with every sort of diversion, national mourning, national rejoicing, fireworks, flood-lighting, processions, and illuminations. They have to maintain expensive establishments which, like a pleasure-steamer, cost as much when they are empty as when they are full. The solid revenue of radio is unaffected by weather or by any other accident. Their clients, having bought their sets, can sit in their comfortable chairs at home, from

January to December, laughing at the weather and enjoying, very often, on the screen or radio, the public scenes which are emptying the theatre—Princess Margaret at Lime Grove, Pat Smythe jumping, Russian soccer teams, or American boxers. On radio, we would say, if we must fine fun at all, should fall the heaviest charge.

I do not seriously suggest that comparable taxes be levied on 'the air'. For that would mean that, at the very least—that is, in comparison with the cheapest theatre seats—your radio licence (without television) would cost £312, of which the Treasury would take £46 16*s*. And then, of course, you have to buy your set.

I merely, dear Treasury fellows, wish to make you think.[1]

But then, here is:

(*b*) THE CINEMA CASE

(From a document sent to Members of Parliament in 1956 by the Cinematograph Exhibitors Association of Great Britain and Ireland.)

Crisis in the British Film Industry

'For the past ten years or more the British Film Industry has been in a state of constant financial difficulty. As Members of Parliament have stated in the course of many debates on the Industry, it has passed from one crisis to another.

'These crises have been temporarily eased, partly by the Industry's own efforts and partly by Government assistance.

'Cinema exhibitors have offset decreasing admissions and falling revenue by miscellaneous sales, etc.,[2] entirely unrelated to their real purpose of providing public entertainment.

'Film producers have only been saved from financial collapse by such palliatives as loans from public funds, or

[1] It seems that we have. See page 169—Mr Harold Macmillan.

[2] e.g. ice-cream.

by such schemes as the British Film Production Fund, by which, at the Government's suggestion, the proceeds of a voluntary[1] levy on practically all cinema admission tickets were made available to British Film Producers.

'What is the reason for this continuous state of crisis in an industry which has become part of the British way of life, and which provides entertainment for nearly 25 million of the population every week?

'The seed of the crisis was sown nearly forty years ago, during the 1914-18 War, when the then Chancellor, Mr Reginald McKenna, clapped a tax on tickets sold at the cinema box office.

'The tax, which was described as Entertainments Duty, was imposed "as a temporary measure, to be abolished when the 1914-18 War was won".

'But today—forty years after—the girl in the cinema box office is still a tax-collector. Not only have successive Governments failed to implement this pledge, but they have increased the rate of Entertainments Duty on a number of occasions until, by 1954, the Chancellor was collecting the huge revenue of 32·6 per cent of gross takings, or 50·3 per cent of net takings, at the cinema box office.

'After the Second World War, as a result of this burden of taxation, of falling cinema admissions, and of steadily increasing production and operating costs, it was the British Film Producer who first felt the chill wind of financial crisis. He was only saved from complete disaster by Government intervention.

'But in the past few years the crisis has spread to all sections of the Industry.

'Many cinema exhibitors, particularly the smaller ones, are now making a loss. Some are being forced to close;

[1] This, under the Cinematograph Films Bill introduced by the Government late in 1956, is to be made statutory and compulsory 'at a somewhat higher rate'. There were hints—but hints only—of consequential concessions on Entertainments Duty (see House of Lords debate, December 20, 1956).

others are covering costs only by miscellaneous income derived from ancillary sales, etc.

'The position of the distributors is also far from satisfactory in that the sharp increase in their operating expenses has not been matched by an expanding volume of sales.

'In the Finance Act of 1954, the Chancellor of the Exchequer recognized the growing difficulties of the British Film Industry and cut £3½ million from the £37·4 million load of taxation on the industry.

'But the cut was too small. Even this moderate reduction in tax was not realized—and the remaining burden (in 1954, £35·9 million out of gross box office takings of £110 million) is still crippling the Industry.

'In the coming year the whole British Film Industry will face a major crisis. And it is for this reason that the four Associations of the Industry—the Association of Specialized Film Producers, the British Film Producers Association, the Cinematograph Exhibitors Association, and the Kinematograph Renters Society—set up an All-Industry Tax Committee to make a complete examination of the financial state of the Industry as a whole.

'This Committee, under independent Chairmen drawn from leading firms of chartered accountants, have now concluded their examination, and have submitted to the Chancellor of the Exchequer a case for a reduction in Entertainments Duty on behalf of the whole Film Industry of Great Britain.

'It must be remembered that the interests and needs of the various sections of the Industry are not always identical but the overwhelming necessity for tax relief is apparent from this unanimous submission to the Chancellor.

'The All-Industry Tax Committee Reports on the Present Circumstances of the Industry

'The cinema is an established feature of the British way of life. In 1954, 1,276 million people went to the cinema, nearly 25 million each week.

'Enormous though this figure may seem it is 359 millions less than in 1946, for since that year the trend of admissions has been downward, and since 1954 markedly so. In 1946 attendances were 1,635 million; in 1954 the corresponding figure was 1,276 million. The downward trend has continued in 1955 and accelerated.

'There are some 4,500 cinemas in Great Britain, of which 2,048 have a capacity of 750 seats or less. The average gross admission price has only been increased during the years 1946-54 from 17·3 pence to 20·7 pence, i.e. by 3·4 pence, while the net admission price (after deducting Entertainments Duty and British Film Production Fund Levy) only went up from 11·1 pence to 13·4 pence, i.e. by 2·3 pence.

'Entertainments Duty was collected from the box office to the extent of 32·6 per cent of gross takings or 50·3 per cent of net takings in 1954 and amounted to £35·9 million. In 1955, after the small reduction in the 1954 Finance Act, it still totalled £33·7 million.

'Entertainments Duty is in no way a tax on profits: it is payable by exhibitors even if their cinemas are trading at a loss and is in part borne by the producer of the film exhibited whether or not that film has recovered its cost of production.

'It is pertinent to point out that, as the Industry understands it, this Duty was conceived as a levy on the consumer, but the trend of business has been such that it is now, in fact, borne by the Industry itself. This duty might not be such a heavy burden if it were relatively small in amount, but at its existing level its effect is crippling.

'There is a further grave disadvantage, peculiar to Entertainments Duty, that its imposition by reference to fixed groups of admission price levels makes it extremely difficult for the Industry to adjust seat prices in relation to fluctuating expenses.

'As the scale at present exists there is insufficient flexibility to meet the impact of rising costs especially as it affects the lower-priced seats. For example, *if the price of 1s. seat (tax 1½d.) were increased to 1s. 6d. (tax 5½d.) the Exchequer collects an additional 4d., the British Film Production Fund an additional ¼d., and the Exhibitor an additional 1¾d.*

'The existing high rates of Entertainments Duty had their origin in the war years when cinemas were packed to capacity. Since 1946 there has been a steady decline in admissions, coupled with increasing costs common to all businesses, and in a period of general prosperity the film industry has failed to retain its share of the national personal expenditure.

'In comparable conditions the Government of the United States has recognized this change and reduced its rate of Admission Tax from 20 per cent to 10 per cent (seats up to 50 cents—equivalent to 3*s.* 9*d.*—being tax free). Entertainments Duty in the United States now represents 9 per cent of the gross box-office receipts as compared with 32 per cent in this country. If expressed in the way which is common in the United States, the tax in Great Britain amounts to 50·3 per cent of net box-office receipts compared with 10 per cent in the U.S.A.

'The deterioration in the financial position of the British Film Industry since 1946 is also due partly to the competition of other forms of personal expenditure; and in recent years to the powerful competition of television services. In 1956 the Industry will have to face the enormously increased competition of television as reinforced by the Independent Television Authority.'[1]

And here are some 'human' details from the manager of a small cinema:

[1] In the autumn of 1956 Mr J. Arthur Rank announced the closing of 79 cinemas 'because they are making losses'. Sir Tom O'Brien, M.P., general secretary of the National Association of Theatrical and Kine Employees, said that he believed 'that well over 1,000 cinemas would have to close within the next two years, unless the Government gave a major relief in entertainment tax' (*The Times*, 13 September 1956). Mr Rank's company said, 'This decision has been taken because of the absence of any entertainment tax relief in the last Budget. . . . The cinemas have been kept open in the hope of tax relief.'

'Recently I was glad to read in your paper[1] a slight protest over Entertainment Duty affecting small cinemas, of which hundreds are now being forced to close down through over-systematic taxation.

'Look at my figures:

	Cinema profit			*Tax*		
	£	*s.*	*d.*	*£*	*s.*	*d.*
1953	52	8	1	2,589	17	4
1954	77	18	2	2,784	5	9
1955	12	18	11	2,882	9	3

1956 Admission 3 per cent down and in the red after tax.

'For working seven days a week, many, many hours a day, the only profit I have by the way of salary has been £300-£400 on sale of ice-cream and chocolates.

'After 10 years of paying nearly £3,000 a year in tax I am trying to sell this modern cinema, 25 years old, for any industrial purpose. Our 10,000-12,000 local inhabitants, who for a quarter of a century have had pleasant, clean entertainment will now go without.

'Tax has closed four cinemas in Nottingham—Bulwell Palace, Boulevard, Queens, and Cosy, Netherfield. More will follow, and this is going on all round the country.

'Last week I showed *A Town Like Alice*, and after 2,256 admissions the result was another loss on the week. Look who gets what:

	£	s.	d.		£	s.	d.
Net takings	135	13	5	Tax	£61	8	3
Expenses	105	0	0				
Film Hire	36	10	0				
	141	10	0				

Loss £5 16*s.* 7*d.* with nothing for self.'

[1] *Daily Express.*

(*c*) THE FOOTBALL CASE

This is not so complicated. At least, there is no Zoo-Clause or Eady Scheme. In the original Act football, with all other games, was taxed at the same rate as the theatre. Football (supported by the Labour Party) thinks it should be still. For a period (1948–52) it was: but in 1952 Mr Butler, creating his three-story 'Tax Structure', brought horse, dog, and motor-racing down to the second story, and sent games and sports up one floor to join them, leaving the living theatre alone on the ground floor. This meant that the football tax was doubled. Mr Butler (1953) added insult to injury by exempting cricket altogether—and other games when played by amateurs.

'It was indeed a shock,' wrote the Football Association, 'when the Government decided that Association football is not played by human beings. A remarkable difference was made between this game and other forms of "live" performances. . . .

'If W. Watson of Yorkshire plays for England at cricket he plays as a professional in a match that is exempted from Entertainments Duty, but if he plays for England at Association football, he is a professional and for that reason that match must carry Duty at the higher rate.'

Isn't it fun?

The Football Association is the controlling body for all 'soccer', professional and amateur. The Football League controls the 92 senior professional clubs, and here is (in part) the claim it submitted in 1956:

'. . . The Treasury have been made aware of the tremendous financial responsibilities of Football Clubs, the provision of wages, the upkeep of grounds, travelling expenses, etc. The Treasury is aware too that most clubs are Limited Companies with Shareholders and Directors and that no Directors' Fees are permitted. It has been stressed also that it is to the interest of the Treasury that Football Clubs should continue to function in view of the large revenue received annually from Football Pools.

'Football, however, unlike Cricket, still bears the burden of this Duty. The position is getting more and more desperate, we know of Clubs which are only kept in existence by the Directors' private purses, or by some source outside football. We know of other Clubs where the Directors have personally signed guarantees at the Bank for considerable sums and others where the Players have voluntarily cut their wages to keep the Club going.

'In a further attempt to secure the removal of this unjust and gradually strangling burden we submit a list showing the Profit or Loss of each of the 92 League Clubs in England and Wales for their last financial year, together with the amount each Club has paid in Entertainment Duty during the same period.

'This shows a total of £900,508 paid in Entertainment Duty by the Clubs over the period. Over the same period 54 of the Clubs incurred considerable losses, and in all but 4 cases where profits were made the amount of Entertainment Duty paid far exceeded any such profits. Here are striking examples. Plymouth Argyle paid £13,488 in Entertainment Duty and their profit was £306. Again the Chelsea Football Club in three years paid £78,000 in Entertainment Duty and during the same period made an overall profit of £34,000. That is to say the Chelsea Club paid in Duty alone £2 7*s.* for every £1 profit, and the West Bromwich Albion Football Club in the last three years has paid £62,000 in Entertainment Duty, and during the same period made a total profit of £19,500. This represented more than £3 to the Exchequer and £1 to the Club.

'These examples are not unusual: they are general and typical. It is no wonder the Clubs regard Entertainment Duty as an imposition and an unjust burden on an enterprise whose sole object is to provide outdoor recreation and entertainment to masses of people in every industrial area in the country.

'Football therefore urges the Chancellor in his Budget proposals to remit this Tax and so ease a burden on Clubs which has become more and more difficult to bear. We do not know how much the Exchequer benefits from this Duty but it cannot much exceed £1,000,000 per annum, from Football, but in the collecting of it, which is done incidentally by the Clubs at no cost whatever to the Treasury, previous Chancellors have built up considerable opposition throughout the country. We therefore plead with the Chancellor to give to Professional Football that relief which his predecessor has given to Professional Cricket.'

And here are some examples of tax plus loss which remind me of the theatre world:

Club	*Profit*	*Loss*			*Duty paid*		
	£	£	*s.*	*d.*	£	*s.*	*d.*
		Division 1					
Birmingham City		11,454	0	0	13,581	0	0
Preston North End		13,579	0	0	15,864	0	0
Tottenham Hotspur		4,505	0	0	25,875	0	0
		Division 2					
Bury		6,572	8	2	9,083	14	4
Middlesbrough		13,032	6	7	11,292	10	6
Sheffield Wednesday		12,384	0	0	15,137	0	0
		Division 3 (South)					
Bournemouth & B.A.		5,911	15	7	7,068	3	1
Crystal Palace		15,908	3	3	6,826	11	6
Southampton		10,700	10	11	9,295	7	10
		Division 3 (North)					
Bradford City		5,082	0	0	4,791	2	6
Darlington		1,127	3	4	3,656	13	8
Grimsby Town		6,668	13	1	6,070	4	9

1956—THE POISON AT WORK

On 2 June, a fortnight before the Committee stage of the

Finance Bill, the able and charming Labour Member, Mr J. P. W. Mallalieu, contributed an article to the *New Statesman and Nation*, which at last showed the Levy poison at work in the open—and the frightening force of honest error.

He began well enough: 'There is some case for the abolition of the tax', and gave some of the good old reasons. He mentioned the 'disquieting anomalies' produced by the Zoo-Clause, and, from personal experience, objected to the 'arbitrary powers' which the Customs and Excise ought not to have and are not fitted to use. But then, because of the Arts Council 'concession' argument and the Levy argument about 'benefiting the landlords' he concluded: 'I would prefer to keep the tax and the exemption from it on non-distributing companies, but to take all discretionary power away from the Customs and Excise.'[1]

The sinister thing was that this man of goodwill had evidently been utterly misinformed about the working of the Zoo-Clause. 'I thought', he confessed to me on the telephone, 'that when a "non-profit" company was exempt from tax the tax was still collected but handed over to the company'! The debate was just ahead and this was an important Labour scribe in the chief Labour organ of opinion. 'Chase every hare.' Bill Linnit arranged for two or three replies, but only a wordy one of my own got in. In it I exposed publicly for the first time the 'infamous argument' of the Arts Council. It was worth the effort. Mr Mallalieu, an honest man, came round.

[6]

IN COMMITTEE, FINANCE BILL, 1956

Though the Levy poison was, in the end, ejected by the Labour Party, the doubts and delay which it produced caused the official Party amendment to be low in the list, and therefore late in the debates.

[1] Stage 6—see page 63.

First, on 13 June, came the cinema, and four new Clauses were debated together. They sought relief, chiefly, for the cinema with 'small weekly takings', and were ably championed by Mrs Eirene White.[1] She frankly mentioned, as others did, 'the counter-attraction of Television', which sat sniggering in the Gallery throughout the debate. The cinema, which has done so much to damage, but not defeat, the theatre, is now in fear of one more new mechanical upstart. In 1916 the 'picture palace' was the main excuse for introducing the tax: in 1956 it is still (because of the revenue it brings—some £30,000,000) the main excuse for continuing the tax. So theatre folk have no great cause to sympathize with 'the movies', and yet, because they are, like the theatre, alliances of all the arts, and, without doubt, 'partly educational', we must. (See page 150—Case for the Cinema.)

Mr Henry Brooke (Financial Secretary) replied for the Treasury (Vol. 554, col. 1313). At the end there was the usual stuff about 'reviewing the whole affair' which the Treasury has been churning out since the days of Neville Chamberlain, 21 years ago:

'. . . We have set on foot a thorough-going review of all sections of the Entertainments Duty. . . . The Chancellor has reached the conclusion that this year, when he has had to introduce a firm—and some would say, severe—Budget to prove our national determination to surmount the difficulties of the time, it would be quite out of keeping to announce reductions of any kind this year in the Entertainments Duty. However . . . my right hon. Friend is not permanently content with all the existing rates and arrangements of the Entertainments Duty as they stand. He considers that they are going to require further attention.'

Mr Macmillan himself said (col. 1341):

[1] Vol. 554, col. 1273.

'Sir Tom O'Brien speaks with perfect truth when he says that, in the present situation, the whole problem of the Entertainments Duty would have to be reconsidered in the light of new developments. That is true. . . .'

He felt that 'the surplus in the present conditions, this year, should be fortified rather than dissipated'. But, 'We will look at the whole structure of Entertainments Duty. Many changes may have to take place' (col. 1342).

(I carefully record this new set of undertakings, that they may be easily accessible to all next year.)

After that there was no hope for anyone. But on 25 June Mr Ellis Smith doggedly moved to exempt games and sports—other than racing. He was defeated by 226–173. Football, and Rugby League Matches, went into the lobby too, with no better fortune. (See page 156—The Football Case.)

On 26 June the theatre was reached and Dr Barnett Stross (Labour) moved a new Clause:

'*Exemption of certain performances from Entertainments Duty*

'(1) Entertainments duty shall not be chargeable in respect of any entertainment where all the performers whose words or actions constitute the entertainment are actually present and performing and the entertainment consists solely of one or more of the following items, namely, a stage play, a ballet, a performance of music or a music-hall, or other variety entertainment.

'(2) This section shall have effect, and be deemed to have had effect, as regards payments for admission to entertainments held on or after the sixth day of August, nineteen hundred and fifty-six, other than payment made before the sixth of August in that year.

'(3) In this section the expression "stage play" has the meaning assigned to it by section twenty-three of the Theatres Act, 1843.

'(4) In relation to entertainments to which this section applies, subsection (2) of section fifteen of the Finance Act,

1950 (which provides for the reduction of entertainments duty in certain cases), shall have effect as if after the word "rates" in that subsection there were added the words "or not at all".' (Vol. 555, col. 324)

Of all the uncountable debates about the Duty this, though it ended in the usual negative, may prove to have been one of the most effective. The case rolled in upon the Treasury Bench with the accumulated force of years, not the seventh but the seventieth wave. Certainly the fight the Members put up was heartening to those behind the lines, to Dingle Foot, Christopher Powell, 'Bill' Linnit and others, who for so many months—the best part of a year—had been patiently at work outside. All the ammunition was ready to the willing hand.

Dr Barnett Stross made a very able speech about 'this deadly, murderous tax'. He said, 'The theatre is in a state of decline' and paraded the latest evidence—80 provincial theatres closed in the past few years—fewer plays and smaller casts, orchestras scarcer and smaller—fewer shows on tour—unemployment in the acting profession 13 per cent against the national figure of 1 per cent.

It is an old rule of dramatic writing that if you have anything important to say you must say it, somehow, at least three times (because of possible coughs and other distractions).

And here is Dr Stross still shouting the point of principle which I was shouting in 1935, 21 years earlier (Vol. 555, col. 325):

'. . . 14 per cent or 15 per cent on turnover. The relevant word is "turnover" and that is why with some confidence I say that this is a thoroughly bad tax for it is a tax not on the profits of the individual theatre but on its turnover.

'There is a tax on the turnover of this industry while its most recent and formidable competitor, commercial television, receives a substantial subsidy of £750,000 a year for ten years, with additional capital advances of up to £2 million. We have the interesting situation that a well-tried instrument of culture has been savagely attacked by taxation since 1916, while a new method of offering news, recreation and perhaps culture too, receives a substantial subsidy at the expense of the taxpayer. . . .

(col. 326) '. . . In 1955 the Golders Green Hippodrome paid £28,250 in taxation. The Streatham Hill Theatre was closed throughout the war owing to war damage and it was opened again in December 1950. Since that time it has paid £60,000 in taxation. Since 1939 that theatre has not dispersed any dividends, has paid no interest on its debentures and has given no fees to its directors. Obviously it is not difficult to accept the cry of distress from the directors of these two theatres when they say that if this taxation continues both theatres must close. . . .

'I should like to give two or three more figures for the six weeks ended on 2 June this year. They are the latest abstract of figures. The Golders Green Hippodrome made a net loss of £650 and during that time the tax paid was £1,437. Streatham Hill Theatre made a net loss of £1,980 and paid tax of £824. . . .'

Dr Stross fairly explained the Levy doctrine, but only to reject it. He read an important letter from Commander Powell, Secretary of The Theatres Entertainment Tax Committee (col. 328):

'Mr Linnit has asked me to let you know that at today's meeting of the Theatrical Managers' Association an assurance was given by those responsible for running the great majority of the larger theatres in the provinces that if the tax were abolished they would be quite prepared to adjust their sharing terms so as to ensure that the non-profit-distributing touring repertory companies would not in any way be the worse off. This may help to allay any anxiety which may be expressed in the debate on their behalf.'

This letter torpedoed the 'manager' side of the Arts

Council's case ('whose attitude is neutral'), and, as for authors' royalties, Dr Stross said, fairly enough (col. 329):

'We who are interested in authors and artists should not find it very objectionable if authors found themselves slightly better off as a result of the abolition of the tax. . . ."

Then there was a queer passage. The Arts Council expected that they would lose, by abolition . . . 'something appreciably less than £20,000 a year. The total figure represented in this matter is just a little over £2 million. Naturally, if this change goes through the Arts Council wants to be reimbursed. If it were to be reimbursed I can assure the Committee that the Arts Council would be in favour of the abolition of the tax.'

Thank you very much. 'Of all the impudence'! Sir Beverley Baxter (Conservative), well-known critic and (once, at least) a playwright, eloquently seconded (col. 330):

(col. 331) 'The footlights are going out one by one all over the country. . . .

'. . . The living theatre supplies the continuing story of our speech and thought through the centuries. If there had been no such thing as the printed word, the theatre itself would have told the continuing story of our people. One Chancellor after another recognizes this to be true but somehow does nothing, or so little that the process of decline and fall goes on. . . .

(col. 332) '. . . The theatre is in this absurd situation: if only one person turned up and bought a ticket—perhaps for one of my plays—and no other ticket was sold, the lean fingers of the Treasury would take part of the money.'

Mr Gordon Walker: 'Mean fingers.'

Sir B. Baxter: 'The lean, grasping fingers of the Treasury would take part of the price of that one ticket. . . .'

'Why not take action now? Why not give the theatre a chance to survive in an age when most of our people, as far as entertainment goes, have forgotten what the human voice really sounds like? They get nothing but animated photography in the form of films or television, a recorded voice. They hardly ever hear the glorious language spoken, as it was intended to be spoken, by human beings.'

Dr King (Labour) and Miss Joan Vickers (Conservative) made good speeches. Mr Mallalieu (Labour) confessed that 'until a very short time ago' he had been in danger of yielding to the 'non-profit' argument, but now saw his way clear: and I was glad that I had troubled to write to the *New Statesman.*

My old colleague, Sir Herbert Butcher (Nat. L. and C.) said:

(col. 342) 'I believe that the retention of this tax is an absolute loss to the national Exchequer as a whole in the widest and broadest sense. During the last year, 80 theatres, perhaps more, have closed. They were theatres that were paying rates, consuming light, encouraging public transport and selling excisable liquors and tobacco on which revenue duties were obtained; theatres which were employing people who were making their own contribution to the National Insurance Fund for health and unemployment benefits and who were earning incomes on which tax was paid. Those theatres have closed, and all that revenue has been lost to the nation as a whole. . . .'

Mr Jeger (Labour), a theatre manager himself, usefully said something for the 'bricks and mortar men', who are generally supposed to be 'sitting pretty' and robbing everyone (col. 344):

'The cost of running a theatre has increased tremendously. There are increased wages all round, increased costs of equipment, of lighting and of rates since the new assessments came into operation. Very often theatre owners cannot afford to keep their theatres in the state in which they should be if they are to compete successfully with modern cinemas and with television at home. . . .'

But the Financial Secretary (Mr H. Brooke) lengthily said the customary No (col. 350):

'We cannot monkey about with different parts of the Entertainments Duty.' (God save us!) 'If there were to be an alteration here, in fairness it would be necessary to re-examine all the rest of the structure of the Entertainments Duty and to bring forward more far-reaching proposals.' (col. 351.)

Here is a queer passage, a little Treasury masterpiece:

(col. 353) '. . . It is interesting to analyse the sources from which the £2 million of revenue come. We have investigated this very carefully and in broad figures about three-quarters of that sum—about £1½ million—comes from variety and musical shows and not more than one-quarter—that is, £500,000—from what we call the straight theatre. If, therefore, the tax were removed, the major advantage would accrue to productions of this type of variety shows. I say that not for one moment to denigrate them, or depreciate their undoubted attractions, but simply to get this matter into perspective. This plea for exemption of tax, which is so often put to the public as a plea for the relief of culture, is, in fact, a plea to a large extent for removing a burden of tax from the seaside variety show. . . .'

The '£1½ million', observe, first comes from 'variety and musical shows', which includes everything from John Gay, Sheridan, and Gilbert and Sullivan to Coward, Novello, *Oklahoma*, *Bless the Bride*, and revue: but in the last sentence it comes from 'the seaside variety show'.

(I give the gentleman at the Treasury who devised this argument full marks: but I should like as well, in case he is tempted to use it again, to draw his attention to the following passage from a book by the distinguished critic of the *New York Herald Tribune* Mr Walter Kerr:

'It is interesting to note that, of all the forms of our time, musical comedy is the only one to make use of: free, unrealistic backgrounds; rapid leaps through time and space; bold color; heightened language (in its lyrics); rhythm (in its music); dynamic movement (not only in its dance, but everywhere); direct address to the audience. Musical comedy is the form that makes the most extensive use of theatrical convention in our time, and something of its theatrical vitality must stem from the fact. The form is eager to please its audiences, and to explore the theatre as theatre—*two things that the serious drama has not thought of doing in quite a long while.* We generally regard the popularity of musicals as a sign of public illiteracy; it may actually be a response to creative joy.'[1]

But Mr Brooke, though colder, was clearer than his chief in some ways (col. 355):

'. . . The Chancellor has authorized me to repeat that he is not satisfied with the structure of Entertainments Duty as it stands; and does not think that it ought to remain indefinitely as it operates at present. He is re-examining the whole matter, in connection not only with the living theatre but the cinema and sports and games of all kinds. . . .'

Mr Gordon Walker (Labour) (col. 356):

'. . . He said that we cannot monkey about with Entertainments Duty. I do not see how he can say that when so many extraordinary anomalies exist in this duty at present, in connection with partly educational, profit-making and non-profit-making productions. This tax has been monkeyed about with already, and is now riddled with anomalies. . . .

(col. 357) '. . . . I knew that the right hon. Gentleman would say that the Chancellor does not want to kill the theatre. He said the same thing about sport. He is like the Quaker sea captain who captured a pirate and told him

[1] From *How Not to Write a Play* by Walter Kerr, p. 237 (Simon & Schuster, N.Y., 1955).

that his principles forbade him killing the pirate, but he would hold the pirate's head under water until it pleased the Lord to take his life away. That is the attitude of the Chancellor to the theatre. He is not killing it; he is letting its life run away because he is holding its head under water. The Financial Secretary's argument is a really miserable one . . .'

Sir Thomas O'Brien (Labour) (col. 361):

'. . . The Federation of Theatre Unions, of which I am the President, representing the British Actors' Equity, the Association of Musicians and Variety Artistes, and my own union, the Stage Technicians and Staffs, are convinced that we are not playing the "bosses" game in trying to bring about the abolition of this tax so that there may be more profits for the "bosses". . . .

(col. 362) '. . . The abolition of the duty for the theatre is a surgical operation. The patient is in desperate straits and only a surgical operation can save him . . . .'

Mr Reader Harris (Conservative), Mr Chuter Ede (Labour), Mr A. E. Hunter (Labour), and Mr Moyle (Labour) joined in: and then the Chancellor replied to the storm. They say that he was very tired, and the speech shows signs of it. But it was an almost moving rendering of an ancient air, the agony of a Chancellor who aches to make a concession but must not (col. 373):

'Look at the broad picture,' he said, 'within which I have had to work this year. . . . I have budgeted for a Budget surplus of £450 million. I have made increases of £30 million in direct taxation and £27 million in indirect taxation. I have made no remissions. I thought it my duty to make none, though it is always much easier and more popular to do so. I made no remissions nor recommended any to the Committee. . . .'

But everybody, of course, asks for remissions. '. . . The smallest ones are, perhaps, the most difficult. The argument is, "It is not a very big thing; it will not cost very much. It is rather mean to resist it. . . ."

'. . . Today, we come to the one which, I am bound to say, presents the strongest and best argument of all—the living theatre. We are told that only about £1½ million is involved; it will not affect the Budget. No one of these, of course, or, indeed, two or three, would affect the mathematical balance of the Budget or what the surplus will be next year. It will not do that. . . .

'Nor would I try to argue that I am satisfied with the Entertainments Duty as I find it. It was created during the war and carried on by Chancellors of the Exchequer after the war. It has a great many difficulties and anomalies in it. It is a tax on a great many different kinds of entertainment, and, meanwhile, there have grown up different rival forms of entertainment which have created quite a new situation. I think that there may even be anomalies there in that some of these entertainments—I mean the new ones—are not so heavily taxed as others. . . .'

(This was, I think, the first official reference to the point I had been making in the papers—the measurement by time—1*s.* in the £ an hour on the theatre, but 26 hours of radio for 1*d.*, etc.—see page 149.)

And here, in full, are the Chancellor's final remarks, for they may one day be described as an historical point in this long struggle. At all events, they have raised high hopes and deserve to be studied closely—not only for the hopes but the hedges in between (col. 375):

'. . . I will be absolutely frank with the Committee as I have been throughout. I have great sympathy with the case which has been put and I do not pretend that if this concession were granted it would overthrow the balance of the Budget. At the same time, I have resisted all the claims put forward for the same reasons, and I must ask the Committee to do so on this broad, general ground.

'I do not think that it would be fair for me to select this

one or that one. We are engaged in a very difficult operation. Perhaps it will succeed; perhaps it will fail. I believe that it will succeed. My hopes for this year may prove illusory—I do not know—but I believe that there is a great measure of agreement in our country, perhaps greater than ever before, about some of the broad problems that confront us as a people. I believe that we are going to succeed. Even with all these cases of one kind and another—sport, Association football, the Rugby League, and the living theatre—I do not want to disturb the broad theme of the Budget.

'If this were a Budget in which tax concessions were being made—and I have made none except in the field of savings, which has a quite different purpose—I could not resist some of the claims which have been so well argued. But that is not the theme of the Budget. It is in that sense austere because of the inflationary situation which we are trying to meet. I believe that we will overcome it, but I will say this. I certainly will look very carefully at the structure of the Entertainments Duty as a whole. I think that it will have to be remodelled.

'Ministers have their duty to do, but I do not believe that in its present form this tax can stand up to the serious criticism that is levelled against it. It will be a strong claimant for some relief when the time comes for relief, and I hope that that may be in the next Budget.'

Mr John Rankin (*Glasgow, Govan*): 'Is that a promise?'

Mr Macmillan; 'I shall come to that.

'I do not think that the Entertainments Duty as such, which brings in £40 million, is necessarily a very high claimant for total remission. There are much higher claimants than that when it comes to giving benefits or reduction of taxation. I do not think that the hon. Gentleman would claim it. Certain parts of it require refashioning and remodelling and certain parts could not sustain that examination; and this would apply particularly, I think, to the theatre. *The tax as a whole is a big contributor to our taxation and it must be broadly sustained.*

'Therefore, I give this pledge and I state it quite deliberately. I hope that this will be the last occasion on which it will be necessary for me or for Treasury Ministers to defend the tax upon the living theatre, or, indeed, the Entertainments Duty in its present form.

'When I say that it is a pledge, I am a careful man. I am fighting as hard a battle—I have had six months of it—as any man has taken on. We are going to succeed and I will not pledge except to say that when the time comes, as I believe it may well come next year, for making relaxations, instead of this austere building up of a surplus and building it even higher, there are certain parts of this tax, of which the one we have been discussing today is a high claimant, which I will certainly see is part of that general reorganization. That, I am sure, we can do.

'I ask the Committee, however, following the very broad lines which I have taken throughout the debate, which are not easy always to sustain against powerful arguments on an individual case, to accept them to the end and to let the example which we have made by this whole financial business this year be one which will be followed through the country and will succeed in its broad purpose.'

Question put, That the Clause be read a second time:

The Committee divided: Ayes, 206: Noes, 243.

A majority of 37 only, as Mr Harold Wilson observed when he 'moved to report progress'. Mr Wilson asked for 'the establishment of an independent committee of inquiry' (he even, rather rashly, used the words 'Royal Commission') 'into the whole system of Entertainments Duty'.[1] The Chancellor drily replied that the appointment of a Royal Commission might postpone a decision for two or three years. He said, too, that he was not 'frightfully attracted by the idea of a Departmental committee'. Instead, he said:[2]

'I undertake to enter into a complete review of this tax and if, God willing, it is my duty to present the result to the

[1] Vol. 555, col. 382. [2] Vol. 555, col. 383.

House, I propose to keep the inquiry in my own hands and to take charge of it myself. That I will do, and I will see that that inquiry is set about forthwith.'

The *Hansard* reader may be puzzled by this, for he may remember that, only seven days earlier, on 19 June, the Financial Secretary, Mr Brooke, said:[1]

'. . . In my speech in the Budget debate, on 19 April, I said that we had set on foot a thorough-going review of all sections of the Entertainments Duty. In order to prove that was not a mere window-dressing argument, I thought of bringing along to the Committee visible proof of the outcome of this review up to date, but because of its comprehensiveness, which would double or treble the thickness of the wad of paper which the Financial Secretary has to carry about with him during the time of the Committee on the Finance Bill, I resisted the temptation to do that. . . .'

I find this a little puzzling too. But my explanation is a happy one, that the Chancellor does not trust his Treasury ('a Departmental committee') and is determined to see for himself.

On 13 July, on the Third Reading, the Chancellor referred to his undertaking of 26 June to review the whole structure of Entertainments Duty. 'At my request,' he said, 'the Customs and Excise have already started work on this' (*The Times*).

[7]

A FEW BASE WORDS ABOUT THE TREASURY

Those were warm words of the Chancellor, and sincere, I am sure. Some theatre-folk were inclined to 'throw up their hats': but mine sits firmly on my head. This talk of 'reviewing' and 'remodelling' has a sadly familiar ring, as those who have read no more than 'Sundry Sayings', at the beginning of this account, will know.

'If my resources enable me . . .' 'If conditions are such

[1] Vol. 554, col. 1322.

that . . .' 'If it were an easier time . . .'—there is always the same qualification. And here it is in Mr Macmillan's 'appropriate and proper moment' and 'when the time comes, as I believe it may well come next year, for making relaxations.'

I have no doubt that Mr Macmillan meant what he said. But he is the tool and slave of the Treasury, who know how much easier it is to retain an old tax than to devise and justify a new one. He will be a hero, indeed, if he persuades them to let this Duty go: and by next year—who knows?—some new crisis may come to their aid, as it has so often before. There may even be, once more, a new Chancellor, not bound by his predecessor's 'pledge'.[1]

I was very glad to see that the Chancellor was not 'frightfully attracted' by the idea of a 'departmental inquiry' for I should not trust the Treasury to inquire into the Treasury's record in this affair. It is that den or fortress of brilliant but bloodless men that rules the lot of us, Ministers, Parliament, and all. So I shall laugh heartily if someone says it is unfair to attack defenceless Civil Servants who cannot answer for themselves. It is their Ministers, too often, who 'cannot answer for themselves'. In all the debates from which I have quoted it is only the Chancellor himself, you may have noticed, never the Financial Secretary, who says an occasional kind word or betrays a generous thought. For the Chancellor alone can dare to stray (with careful reservations) from the pure Treasury doctrine—and even he, it is clear, is rapped on the knuckles when he gets back to Downing Street. The Financial Secretary, the underling, can say nothing but what he is told: and from him comes nothing but cold and ingenious obstruction.

The great Salazar said that the test of a good State was whether it behaved like a gentleman. Does the Treasury?

(1) A gentleman stands by his word. Three independent bodies, the theatre, the cinema, and the Football Association, tell the same tale of 1916—how the Chancellor, Mr

[1] This was written some weeks before the Rape of the Canal.

McKenna, assured them, separately, that the tax was 'an emergency measure', and would be removed after the war, and, upon that understanding, requested and received their active co-operation. No voice from the Treasury has ever bothered to reply to this charge, and I am sure that they are much amused when it is mentioned. The only reply could be that at the end of the war Mr McKenna was no longer Chancellor and his rash pledge could not bind his successor. But such an excuse would not be used by any private concern that was proud of its good name—or be accepted if it were. This, after all, is Her Majesty's Treasury, which expects so high a standard of honour in those who have to pay the taxes, and those who collect the taxes for the Treasury. This is the Treasury, so down on 'cheats' and 'dodgers'.

Here is the first charge, then, that the Treasury has no conscience, no sense of honour.[1]

(2) A gentleman, however eager for money, will say that certain ways of getting it are 'against his principles'. In 1926, as we have seen, Mr Snowden said that he disliked the Entertainments Duty 'in principle'. Other Chancellors, it is clear, though they spoke less firmly, have felt the same. But today, thirty years later, Mr Macmillan may admit no 'principle'. He has to say: 'The tax as a whole is a big contributor to our taxation, and it must broadly be sustained.' Sir Kingsley Wood, surrendering on the books and papers tax, would not admit that there was any 'principle' involved, in spite of the famous victories of a century before. This is the modern Treasury again—as long as they yield no point of principle they can keep on any tax indefinitely, or take it off and put it on again. Books and papers were exempted 'at least for the present'.

Here, then, is the second charge, that the Treasury, in pursuit of money, will admit no superior principle.

(3) A gentleman will not say one thing when he means another. A gentleman will not pretend that he is doing

[1] The motorist, I believe, will join me here.

justice and right when in fact he is seeking power for himself. Even a pirate will not waste time and shot on a poor man in a rowing-boat unless he has a sadistic side to him or has grandiose notions about 'ruling the waves'. In this tax affair, all the elaborate apparatus of differentiation, the categories of exemption, the complicated administration of the Zoo-Clause, all the work of the Treasury and the Custom House, the cost of the Customs officers who must visit every place of entertainment weekly (to say nothing of all those forms and rolls of coloured stamped tickets), all they lose on income tax and surtax and unemployment pay, can not be worth the wretched £2,000,000 which is extracted from the living theatre in a single year. The quarry is not worth the shot, and the stalking. The Treasury are not incompetent, and they must, in their secret hearts, agree. Why, then, are they so keen to retain this fiscally negligible tax? Why does poor Mr Brooke, after dropping a little lukewarm word of sympathy for the theatre's troubles, go out of his way to find such new and nonsensical arguments against it as the 'seaside variety show'? Because, if they lose the theatre tax, *they lose power as well*, the power of lofty patronage—and censorship—by tax-exemption under the Zoo-Clause. The Arts Council have the ear of the Treasury, and there are some, I am sure, in that great building who agree with Mr Levy. They are sorry the tax was halved in 1948, was not left at the peak level of 1943. Then, one by one, the 'commercial' fellows could have been compelled, or welcomed, into the 'non-profit' pen—provided, of course, that they produced none but 'serious' plays—a Treasury Empire of Entertainment, excluding only low 'musical comedy and variety'. As it is, boasts Mr Brooke, they are distributing, by way of the Zoo-Clause, a bounty of £600,000 a year to 2,000 organizations. If the tax goes those organizations need be no worse off, as we have seen. But the Treasury and the Customs will lose the power to choose the sheep and the goats, to determine who shall be taxed and who shall go free, to work what the Arts

Council rashly describes as 'a protective tariff'. We have heard of such 'protection' before—in Chicago, in Soho. The Treasury are saying to the theatre; 'Conduct your business in your own way, and you will pay £2,000,000 tax. Conduct it in ours, and we will protect you.' But that is not a proper thing for Her Majesty's Treasury to say, even under their breath. So here is the third charge: The Treasury are behaving like a gangster.

In short, I mildly feel that the Chancellor is right not to be 'frightfully attracted' to a departmental inquiry.

VI

Conclusion

DR DALTON once suggested that Mr Levy, Mr E. P. Smith, and I should join him as a sort of 'working-party' to consider what should be done about the Duty. I have been wondering what I should say if Mr Macmillan did me the honour to ask for my advice about his 'remodelling'. I should have to begin:

'Dear Chancellor, they have been remodelling this tax for forty years. It is like a statue by an amateur sculptor which never gets beyond the clay stage. Hardly a year passes without a lump or two being added to the nose, or a slice removed from its ugly rump. It was thoroughly "remodelled" by Dalton in 1946. Butler remodelled it in 1952. Doesn't it occur to you that if after all these years of remodelling some more remodelling is an urgent need it may mean that the job is beyond the wit of man? The thing is an ugly wreck. Sink it!'

The Chancellor: 'It still yields £40,000,000 a year—£30,000,000 from the cinema alone.'

Me: 'Yes, Sir, but, as I have been crying for 20 years, remodel the betting laws and you will get much more than that from a tax on betting, thoroughly and justly planned.'

The Chancellor: 'I haven't got it yet.'

Me: 'I know you have to think about money, Sir, but I wish for a moment you could give your mind to men—to the liberties of men. The simple citizen says this: "I have an afternoon, or an evening, off; and in this blessed world, by God created but by Man improved, I can use my leisure in many ways. I can go for a walk, or a drive, or sit in the sun: I can look at flowers or study the stars: I can swim, or run races, or box, or play a game. I can read a book, or magazine, a pamphlet or a newspaper. I can listen to the radio—to music, to sport, or an intellectual talk: I can watch the television screen or go to "the movies". I can go to a concert, a theatre, an opera, a museum or a picture gallery. All this, by the way, is a kind of education—a drawing out. When I have enjoyed fine playing or singing, fine batting or riding, I come home refreshed in spirit, eager to excel in my own small world. Why, in this land of liberty, can I not make my own choice from all these pleasures without the interference of the Treasury? "Interference"? Yes—for some are taxed, and some are not. Why should there be a tax if I see the plays of Mr Smith, but not if I read his books? It must be much more difficult and expensive to present a play than to publish a book. What do I care if those fine performers are professionals or amateurs? What is it to me if the "proprietors" distribute their profits or not? What matters to me is—Do they make my leisure a pleasure? If they do, they will pay the income, and the other, taxes. If they do not, they will go out of business. I do not see why they should pay any tax for trying to please me, especially if they fail.

'With this citizen I must agree, Sir. As I said in the House—as I said at the Royal Academy: "What are we here for? Full Employment?" No—that is but a means. The end is Full Enjoyment, the multifarious blessings of the leisure which is the fruit of good and regular labour. Imagine a world without books, newspapers, music, paintings, concerts and operas, plays—on stage or screen—the manifold delight that we draw from those little boxes in the corner of the room, yes, and all the queer games and gatherings, the feats, the fights, the running and the rowing and the riding, that make the nation a multitude of brothers, delighting in the skill, the swiftness, the fortitude of Man, in the power and beauty of horse and hound. These are the pleasures that distinguish us from the savage and the sheep. Without them, it is true, we should have companionship and friendship and love and marriage, good food and drink, and the joys that Nature provides—but so have the savage and the sheep. (Religion, too, no doubt—but then, where would religion be without the arts and graces that adorn it—the language, the music, the painted window and the sculptured stone?) Without these pleasures, Sir, our lives would be nothing, a daily tramp from the bed to the bench and back again.'

The Chancellor: 'What about the pub?'

Me: 'Ah, well, we may call in there—and are heavily taxed for it: of which I do not greatly complain (except that we are taxed too much), for here are the foods of the body, and some say they are poisoned foods. But I am talking of the foods of the mind, the spirit, the soul—of the Bible and *The Times,* of Shakespeare and Tschaikowsky, of the Queen at her Crowning, of Winston Churchill on his 80th birthday, of the National Gallery and the Maritime Museum, of the Royal Tournament and the Trooping of the Colour, of Pat Smythe on Tosca and Gordon Richards on his Derby winner, of Covent Garden and Drury Lane, of Stratford and Sadler's Wells, of Margot Fonteyn and Moira Shearer, of Bannister and Chataway, of Cochran and Charlot and Hitchcock and Korda, of Garbo and Guinness, of Masefield and Malcolm Sargent. You would not tax a ticket for a chair to sit in the sun. But you, Sir, when you ask me to say how I would "refashion and remodel" the Entertainments Duty are asking me, in effect, to tax the sunshine of the soul.

'Well, Sir, my answer is clear: If you tax one of these pleasures, you must tax the lot. Tax the play—and you must tax the book—and the B.B.C.—and *The Times*—and the *Daily Mail.* Tax Edith Evans—and you must tax Pat Smythe (amateur or no). Tax the movies and you must tax TV. Tax the Derby—and you must tax the Boat Race. Tax football—and you must tax cricket. "But how," you cry, horrified, "are we to get such different creatures into the same cage?" The answer, again, is easy. Work out a formula by which you can measure (*a*) the period of enjoyment, (*b*) the price paid, and (*c*) the appropriate tax. For example, the theatre tax (as we have recorded somewhere) is about 1*s*. in the £ per hour, and that might be a useful basis. You could then work out the time the average man spends on enjoying (*a*) *The Times*, (*b*) a book, (*c*) the radio, (*d*) the movies—and so on, and tax accordingly per hour of enjoyment. The Treasury, I am sure, would enjoy these calculations, and the House of Commons could have many a happy All-Night Sitting discussing them.

'But, of course, Sir, I am not being very serious. I doubt if even the Treasury, with all its foul experience, would commit itself to such tedious and tiny calculations. My real answer is this: "Remodel?" No. You cannot remodel a mess. You cannot refashion a bad strawberry. Scrap the lot! Let us all be free and equal. (And, by the way, you must see fair play. You must let the theatres have Sunday too.) But if there are enterprises of undoubted worth that cannot stand up to the battle, let us give them a helping hand, as here and there we do today—from the State, the Arts Council, or the local authority. And may the present Chancellor be the first to come to the Table and say: "Today I make a unique and splendid proposal. No one will be able to say that it favours the rich or unduly cossets the poor: for it will touch the lives of every citizen in the land. I propose to abolish—root and branch, yes, and all the creeping tangle that has grown about it—the Entertainments Duty. Henceforth, in this land there will be No Tax on Thought, No Duty on Beauty, No Levy on Laughter, and No Fine on Fun!" '

Appendix A

'*Who Pays?*'

'Who pays the tax—today?' This is not, in principle, an important question. A purchase (or sales) tax on the Bible, or *The Times*, would be equally barbarous if it were (*a*) passed on to the 'consumer', or (*b*) paid by the producer. Under (*a*) fewer people would be able to buy these 'cunsumer[1] goods': under (*b*) the producers would be less able to produce them. But the question will have some practical importance when the tax is abolished, and here is an answer—or two:

(1) THE MANAGER

(*a*) Whatever was intended forty years ago, there is no doubt that the 'proprietor' is 'paying the tax' today, not because he is 'wealthy' but because he cannot help it. A tax is only paid by the 'consumer' when it can be simply added to the ordinary economic price, like 'another 1*d.* on the beer': but the theatrical managers cannot do that, because the people will not pay. He cannot even adjust his prices to keep pace with the rise in costs—much less add on a tax as well.

Here is a simple illustration in a letter sent to me, unsolicited, by Mr S. G. Dorrill, M.B.E., Managing Director of the New Theatre, Oxford. He enclosed a photostat copy of "the first contract between the New Theatre, Oxford, and the O.U.D.S. (incidentally in my father's handwriting, with corrections by Arthur Bourchier) from which you will

[1] 'There are high taxes on other consumer goods' (*The Times*, in a leading article on the cinema tax).

observe that the O.U.D.S. were able to obtain 7*s.* 6*d.* for a stall back in 1886. Today I charge 8*s.* 6*d.*, from which Entertainments Duty of 1*s.* 2½*d.* is deducted, leaving me with 7*s.* 3½*d.* Of course, it just does not make sense. It could be argued—why don't I charge more to my best seats? My answer is, if I thought I could get it, I would. . . .

'I have now had just over forty years in the theatre business. I still love it as much as ever—am a perishing optimist as to the future—but I sometimes ask myself, if the Government are not prepared entirely to remove the Entertainments Duty, why should I continue to try to uphold the live theatre in this so-called learned city?'

(*b*) Mr Peter Saunders, a London production manager and an enterprising one, who has not been content to import American successes, writes:

(1) 'Seventy-five years ago the price of a stall was 10*s.* 6*d.* Today, on a 15*s.* stall the management receive 12*s.* 8½*d.* It is not true to say that the tax is paid by the "consumer". If the Government put sixpence more duty on cigarettes the price goes up overnight. This is not the case with the theatre.

(2) 'The real trouble goes back to the boom days during the last war, when theatres packed out and inflation shot up. The "wicked theatrical managers" did not take advantage of the circumstances to push theatre seats up. Had they done so a straight play would be £1 a seat, and a musical 30*s.* A production which twenty-five years ago would have been comfortably put on for £500 could cost £5,000 to £6,000 today. Now, of course, it is rather late in the day to rectify the error. The fact that theatre prices have not been put up parallel with the rise in production costs, staff wages, and the sundries that people like to overlook, like the cost of printing, the cost of electricity, the cost of coal, the cost of repairs, and the cost of toilet paper in the toilets, merely underlines the fact that the customer is *not* paying the tax at all. What is really happening is that not only has the theatre manager taken over the payment of the tax, but he is

subsidizing the theatregoer by not putting up the price of seats as he should.

(3) 'It is no good pointing to long runs, and saying how well theatrical managements are doing. The tax is virtually killing all enterprise in theatrical production. In the olden days plays with three and four "sets" and a cast of twenty to thirty were very common. Today, the first reaction of a manager receiving a new script is to look at the fly-leaf and say, "How many sets and how many actors?" The tax is the same whatever the scale of the production.

(4) 'And, in conclusion, if the theatre dies out, God help the people who have to look at television and films performed by actors who have not had stage training!'

(*c*) In my own experience, the cost of production of three big musical plays was

1946	*Big Ben*	£12,000
1947	*Bless the Bride*	£15,000
1955	*The Water Gipsies*	£28,000

(Only one, *Bless the Bride*, showed a profit.)

The price of the most expensive stall was, I think 16*s*. 6*d*. in each case. Of that sum, in 1956, the State abstracted 2*s*. 6½*d*., leaving the manager 13*s*. 11½*d*.

At Daly's Theatre, the great home of musical plays, in 1916 before the tax, the top price of a stall was 10*s*. 6*d*. So after 40 years the manager gets 3*s*. 5½*d*.—about 33 per cent—more. But the cost of producing a 'musical', they say, has risen more than 500 per cent.

(*d*) Mr Prince Littler, C.B.E., on 10 April 1956, sent to the *Daily Telegraph* the following figures about *The King And I*:

'The Theatre Royal, Drury Lane, has just published its accounts for 1955. From its £251,773 admission money, an amount of £38,521 was taken for Entertainments Duty. The profit for the year amounted to £3,157, out of which Profits Tax and Income Tax accounted for £2,866.

'The shareholders receive £3,593 "net", a return of 5 per cent on their money, and in order to pay this dividend the "brought forward" from last year is reduced from £5,600 to £3,900, so that after a year's trading *with one of the most successful musical plays ever produced in London*, the Government received over £38,000 as tax on turnover, plus Profits, Income tax, rates, etc., while the poor shareholders received £3,593 between them. It hardly seems a fair proportion, and, in my opinion, is an unsatisfactory return for such a speculative business as the theatre industry at the present time. . . . The obvious answer is that unless the crippling burden of Entertainments Tax is removed it means that we shall be forced to raise our prices of admission substantially, and this would have been done long ago to meet the constantly rising costs of production, artistes, salaries and staffs generally; except for one good reason, and that is the strong public resistance to any increase in the prices of admission of theatres.'

(Note, by the way, that Mr Littler is one of those managers who are sometimes blamed for 'taking the easy way' and importing established American successes. Even with a big success things are not so 'easy'.)

The picture is very clearly shown by the official tables of 'rates', which are headed thus:

Charge to public Up to:	*Duty*	*Amount retained by Proprietor*
s. d.	*s. d.*	*s. d.*
10 0	1 5½	8 6½
16 0	2 5½	13 6½

The manager fixes a price which he knows, or hopes, the public will pay for a particular seat, whether it be 10*s.* or 16*s.* The State then says: 'Oh, if you charge that you will have to hand over 1*s.* 5½*d.* or 2*s.* 5½*d.*' He cannot then say, 'Oh, then I shall charge 11*s.* 6*d.*—or 18*s.* 6*d.*' because he knows that his public will not pay so much. And, besides, the tax will then be higher still.

For forty years good people have been writing to the papers: 'If the tax is reduced, will the managers undertake, to "pass it on"—like a relief of tax on tobacco or petrol?'

The first answer is 'No'—for, unlike the tax on cigarettes, this tax is paid by the man who provides the 'entertainment', and he has the top title to relief. Nevertheless, in his own interest, he will always keep his prices as low as he can. But 'undertakings'? No. Much must depend on the circumstances of every case. When the tax was reduced in 1948, C. B. Cochran, I know, reduced his prices on some seats but not on others. I do not think that all managers did the same. Why should they? Like the publishers of books, they should be entitled to keep every penny they can coax into the till, partly because, unlike the tobacco shop, they are merchants of art, ideas, and music, and partly because of the special hazards of this particular market.[1]

If I am wrong—once more—why is the tax not levied at Stratford and Covent Garden? And why is there no purchase tax on newspapers and books?

(2) THE AUTHOR

Another person who 'pays the tax' today—and this is not generally realized—is the dramatist, the foundation, as a rule, of the enterprise. The author, today, receives royalty of *x* per cent on the gross takings *less* Entertainment Tax (so, I believe, does any actor who gets 'a percentage' as well as a salary). This is a matter, not of law, but of custom and contract—and even the custom has not always prevailed. I am not sure about the history of this. In my first contract with Sir Nigel Playfair (in 1926), I see, there was no reference to the tax: but it came in a few years later, and the deduction has appeared in all my theatrical contracts since 1929, certainly. Some say, 'But why do you agree to this?' 'Why should you bear the burden of a tax which was intended by Parliament to be paid by the playgoer—not the

[1] See pages 75, 129—Babies.

playwright?' I really do not know the right answer to this. But our compliance shows, I repeat, that we agree with the managers who say that the tax is paid behind the curtain and not in front of it: and, accordingly, as part of 'the management', we bear part of the brunt. Observe that, if the tax is ever abolished, we shall draw our royalties 'on the gross', and the management, to that extent, will be the poorer.

Appendix B

Comparative Rates in 1916, 1936 and 1956

	Inclusive charge to public		*Duty*		*Retained by proprietor*	
	s.	*d.*	*s.*	*d.*	*s.*	*d.*
1916						
All Entertainments	1	0		2		10
	2	6		2	2	4
	5	0		3	4	9
	10	6	1	0	9	6
1936						
(*a*) Living theatre	1	0		1		11
	2	6		4	2	2
	5	0		9	4	3
	10	6	1	8	8	10
(*b*) Other entertainments	1	0		2		10
	2	6		5	2	1
	5	0		10	4	2
	10	6	1	9	8	9
1956						
(*a*) Living theatre	1	0		Nil	1	0
	2	6		2½	2	3½
	5	0		7½	4	4½
	10	6	1	6½	8	11½

(*b*) Sports, etc.	1	0		Nil	1	0
	2	6		6	2	0
	5	0	1	4	3	8
	10	6	3	3	7	3
(*c*) Cinema	1	0		1½		10½
	2	6		11½	1	6½
	5	0	2	2½	2	9½
	10	6	4	9½	5	8½

Appendix C

(A) ILLUSTRATION OF FICTIONAL 'TAX-EQUIVALENT' CONCESSIONS NOW MADE BY DRAMATISTS (AS AN 'ACT OF GRACE') AND IN SOME CASES BY LOCAL MANAGERS:

Weekly takings are £1,000.

Author's royalty is, say, 10 per cent (a high but convenient figure).

If 'sharing terms', the non-profit company and local manager are sharing at, say, 55/45 (but, N.B. 'sharing terms' cases are a minority).

Gross takings	—	£1,000
Less 'tax-equivalent'	—	150
		£850

Author	*Non-Profit Co.*	*Local Manager*
1. Takes £85 (10 per cent on £850 instead of £1,000)	saves £15	
2. Managers, at 55/45, share £850	gets £467 10*s.* + T.E. £150 = £617 10*s.*	gets £382 10*s.*

(B) SUPPOSE (*a*) ENTERTAINMENT TAX ABOLISHED, or (*b*) TAX REMAINS BUT PRESENT 'TAX-EQUIVALENT' CONCESSIONS WITHDRAWN: i.e. ALL CALCULATIONS MADE ON THE GROSS TAKINGS

But 1. Kind author, in proper case, agrees to take lower royalty of 8½ per cent *on the gross;*

	Author	*Non-Profit Co.*	*Local Manager*
Takes 8½ per cent on £1,000	£85	saves £15 (as before)	
2. Kind local manager agrees to share the gross takings at 60/40		gets £600	gets £400

(C) THERE ARE ALSO OPEN TO SOME OF THESE COMPANIES

Arts Council subsidies
and to all, in theory,
Assistance from local authorities under the Local Government Act, 1948 (up to a 6*d.* rate).

Appendix D

A Tax on Newspapers?

To the Editor of the Manchester Guardian.[1]

SIR,—As I have remarked before, there is no distinction in principle between the entertainments tax on drama, music, and the film, and the purchase tax on newspapers, periodicals, and books which was proposed, in vain, by Sir Kingsley Wood in 1940. I played some part in the resistance movement then; and I have felt entitled, more than once, to appeal to the press for its active aid against the existing taxes on intellectual or artistic effort, whether wholly educational or partly entertaining. The response has been disappointing. I can only conclude that such taxes are considered by most of the newspaper proprietors and editors to be sound in principle and practice. So, eager as ever to be helpful, I have been planning the details of a purchase tax on newspapers and periodicals.

First, the rate. Sir Kingsley Wood proposed to levy the tax at 16⅔ per cent, and hoped to raise £3,500,000 a year. The living theatre tax is now as much as 18 per cent on the original price—3*s.* on a seat priced by the manager at 16*s.*; and in the cinema it runs up to 70-80 per cent. The press, which suffers much less than the theatre from bad weather, good weather, fog, snow, sunshine, sickness, childbirth, national rejoicing, or political disturbance, might settle, I think, for 50 per cent. This would, administratively, be more convenient than 16⅔, and at the higher prices of today should yield £10 millions or more. *The Times* would cost 6*d.* (if *The Times* had to pay), the *Manchester Guardian* 4½*d.*,

[1] *The Times*, to my surprise, declined this letter.

the *Daily Telegraph* and the London evenings 3*d*. But, of course, as we are always being told in the theatre, the tax would be 'paid by the consumer', and the proprietors would have nothing to worry about. Some patriotic papers, no doubt, like the *Daily Express*, would gaily pay the tax themselves; and others, less popular, would be compelled to, as, for the most part, the theatres are.

Now for the method of collection. As in the theatre, no doubt, the law would require a stamp to be affixed to every copy sold, which might prove to be a nuisance. But perhaps the papers, like the theatres, would be permitted to enter into a bond to make a true return of their sales and pay the appropriate tax without the use of stamps. The Custom House men would make weekly visits to check the accounts, and cut up rough if there was any delay in payment; the army of unpaid tax-collectors would be greatly increased. But what organ of good will would complain of such trifles?

Then, I suppose, the Treasury would admit some of those enlightened modifications which have made such a charming patchwork of the entertainments duty. Any paper run by a 'non-profit-making body' which could convince the Custom House that its general aims were 'educational' would be exempt from tax; and here, I take it, *The Times* and *Observer* would qualify. Perhaps *The Times* would count as Covent Garden and get a subsidy as well. There might be complaints from other high-minded papers, like the *Manchester Guardian*, the *Daily Telegraph* and the *Sunday Times*, which would claim to be equally educational in purpose. But they do, I believe, seek to 'make a profit', which in the theatre, even under Conservative Governments, is treated as a kind of wickedness; and according to precedent I am afraid they would have to pay.

At the other end of the scale there might be some papers which, because of their low 'education content', would be taxed with special savagery. The tax could be scientifically graded by the Custom House according to the genuine 'news' and education content of each paper per square column. High marks for relief would go, of course, to any paper which gave reverent reports of cricket and horse-racing, much lower marks to those who stooped to dog-racing or the pools. Some papers, like some theatrical producers, might be ambidexterous. The *Guardian* might be profit-making and pay the tax, the *Junior Guardian* 'educational' and exempt. This will madden many but the Treasury won't care.

What place the tax would fill in the 'overall' economic mess—whether it would be a 'worthwhile factor' in 'mopping up inflationary pressure' or a provocation to wage-claims which could only accelerate the inflationary spiral, a wholesome brake on luxury spending, or a crude assault on the near-necessities of civilized existence—I am unable to say. But I am sure that everyone would love it.

And then, sir, there are books. But the Chancellor was a publisher; and we had better not go too far.—Yours, etc.,

A. P. HERBERT

Appendix E

Rents, 'Bricks and Mortar', etc.

THIS is a history of the Entertainments Duty, not of the rights and wrongs of Real Property. But the rent question does keep cropping up in every discussion of the theatre's troubles; and not only the fanatical foe but the feeble friend is heard to say sometimes 'What's the good? It will all go to the landlords.' Many answers to this have appeared, by the way, in these pages, but it may be useful to assemble them here:

(1) 'That would be a good argument against the reduction of tax on any commodity.' (Mr Osbert Peake, M.P., in 1947.)

(2) 'It should be made clear that if the Duty is abolished the whole amount will not accrue to the funds of the theatre, but will be divided between the theatre and the production companies, thereby assisting the theatre to survive with no more than a modest profit and encouraging the production companies to present a wider range and higher class of entertainments.' (The Theatres Entertainment Tax Committee, 1956.)

(3) If anyone sniffs incredulously at (2) let it be recalled that, as things are, under the Zoo-Clause, the owners are perfectly free to behave rapaciously to the 'non-profiteers', but in fact they have voluntarily, and consistently, made some generous arrangements.

(4) 'If it were true that the theatre was suffering under two staggering blows—one a bad system of rents and the other a bad system of Entertainments Duty—the fact that the rent problem still remains to be dealt with would not be an argument against also dealing with the problem of the Duty.' (Mr Christopher Hollis, M.P., 1947.)

(5) The owner does provide something: the State does not. The owner has costly obligations: the State (in the theatre) has not. So 'If I accuse the State of taking £1,700 out of the till every week it is really no answer to say that the theatre owner is taking £500' (A. P. Herbert, 1947.)

(6) The owner is not always 'sitting pretty'. His costs, etc., have risen too. (Mr Jeger, M.P., 1956.) In the provinces there are many complaints of inferior dressing-rooms, etc. Some of the money now filched by the State should certainly go to the improvement of 'bricks and mortar.'

Other 'non-profiteers' say, 'Oh, but the stage-hands, etc., will ask, and get, more pay, and, where we have to pay them, we shall be the poorer'. Well, the stage-staffs and others too will deserve a slice of any cake that is going. But all this is feeble talk. 'The Theatre' is a variegated team. If it gets, not a gift, but justice at last, it must sensibly divide the benefit between all its members: and no doubt it will. Meanwhile, it is madness for the victims, by spitting at each other, to encourage the robber to go on robbing.

Appendix F

Foreign Countries

IN 1916[1] Sir J. D. Rees said in the House: 'I think too much has been made of the difficulties of collection. . . . I believe there were no such difficulties in Petrograd, and the right hon. Gentleman could easily solve this problem by reference to our Ambassador in Russia, who, I am quite sure, would be willing to tell him how this tax is levied in Russia.'

I have been unable to check the accuracy of Sir J. D. Rees' information, for the Soviet Embassy have failed to respond to my inquiries. But it may be that we got this tax from the Russia of the wicked Czars. Other countries, I believe, have followed our example. France began it on 30 December 1916, and the United States—the Embassies inform me kindly—in 1917. Thus one bad custom doth corrupt the world. Let us lead the world again.

[1] Vol. 81, col. 1825.

Appendix G

Motions to Abolish Tax

MOTIONS, ON THE FINANCE BILL, TO ABOLISH THE ENTERTAINMENTS TAX ON THE LIVING THEATRE

Year	Mover	Ayes	Noes
1933	Mr Alfred Denville (Con.)	No Division	
1937	,, ,, ,,	Ayes: 130	Noes: 192
1937	Mr A. Herbert (Ind.)	Ayes: 118	Noes: 207
1938	,, ,,	Ayes: 115	Noes: 191
1939	Mr George Hall (Lab.)	Ayes: 138	Noes: 201
1954	Mr Woodrow Wyatt (Lab.)	No Division	
1956	Dr Barnett Stross (Lab.)	Ayes: 206	Noes: 243

Summary

I. BIRTH AND EARLY LIFE *page* 15

[1] Tax on 'amusements' born in 1916—for war purposes—Alleged undertakings by Chancellor (MR REGINALD MCKENNA) to abolish it after the war—Idea that it was wrong to go to 'amusements' in time of war—Tax mainly aimed at 'the picture palace', with which Mr Tim Healy had 'no sympathy whatsoever'—'These questionable entertainments . . .'.
[2] Hastily devised—and ceaseless tinkering and patching ever since—Original exemptions 'wholly educational' and 'not for profit'—understandable in war but why have Conservatives maintained anti-profit arrangements ever since?—At last moment special paragraph added for protection of the Zoo (which has caused much unforeseen trouble in the theatre)—There are now 12 (or 13) categories of exemption and 3 different scales of tax (see pages 101 and 192).
[3] Original intention—tax should be paid by individual who went to 'amusements' 'at a time like this'—But change in machinery of collection (1916) made it possible for 'proprietors' to pay, and subsequent events have made it inevitable (see Appendix 'A'—'Who Pays?').

II. AFTER THE (FIRST) WAR *page* 24

1920–1935. From 1920 theatre and entertainment folk almost annually sought relief, in vain—In 1932 Sunday Entertainments Act freed Sundays for cinema—1933 Mr Alfred Denville made first proposal to abolish tax on 'living theatre'—1934 MR NEVILLE CHAMBERLAIN said he would like to 'remodel' tax.
1935. Theatre much affected by growth of radio and cinema, both (unlike theatre) able to operate seven days a week—MR NEVILLE CHAMBERLAIN now, for first time, introduced a lower rate for

'living theatre' (including ballet, music-hall and circuses). Rise and Fall of Rates.
1937–1939. Strong support from all parties for motions to reduce or remove the theatre tax—1939—analysis of tax's character, incidence, etc. (A. P. Herbert, M.P.) SIR JOHN SIMON genuinely sympathetic, and in 1939 made a further reduction in rate—But for the war, it is believed, he might have abolished the duty.

III. THE (SECOND) WAR *page* 40

1940. SIR KINGSLEY WOOD—tax increased but differential rate for theatre retained—Tax doubled in 1942—and further increased in 1943, when peak was reached—Theatrical and entertainment folk, said Chancellor, loyally co-operative throughout—they loved it—In 1940 SIR KINGSLEY WOOD proposed to lay purchase tax on newspapers, periodicals, and books, but after strong protests, in and out of Parliament, thought better of it, 'at least for the present'.
1943–1945. SIR JOHN ANDERSON, who succeeded SIR KINGSLEY, had some administrative trouble about 'the Zoo-Clause' and the theatre (see 1946 (*b*)).

IV. AFTER THE (SECOND) WAR *page* 53

1946. 1. DR DALTON (*a*) reduced rate of tax on sport (other than horse, dog, and motor-racing) to lower level of living theatre: (*b*) amended 'Zoo-Clause' (Act of 1916, Section 1 (5) (*d*)—partly educational or scientific entertainments provided by 'non-profit' society)—Enter Mr Benn Levy, M.P.—Strange history of paragraph applied to theatrical entertainments since 1934—Charges of 'tax-evasion' and abuses in 1942, 1943—DR DALTON's present amendment originally proposed by SIR JOHN ANDERSON—Test no longer to be 'partly educational' character of each play, but 'educational aims, etc., of the "non-profit" society'—Row about *A Streetcar Named Desire* in 1949—Arguments for and against 'non-profit' arrangements.

2. Motion by two dramatist Members, A. P. Herbert and E. P. Smith, for tax not to be levied, in theatre, till costs of production paid off, that is, till way to a 'profit' open—Opposed by third dramatist, Benn Levy—Rejected.

1947. Motion by same two dramatist Members to reduce rate to 1939 level—about half. Opposed by same dramatist, Benn Levy, who said theatre tax should be maintained for theatre's good—question of Rent (Mr Peake)—Rejected.

1948. 1. SIR STAFFORD CRIPPS reduced rate on living theatre, etc., to 1939 level, about half (as shyly suggested by two dramatists in 1947).

2. Local Government Act—MR ANEURIN BEVAN gave local authorities power to provide or assist entertainments—disappointing results.

1950. The Cinema—the Eady Levy—and British Film Production Fund.

1952. MR R. A. BUTLER created a new 'Entertainments Duty Structure'—Racing came down—other 'sport' went up—Thus three rates (1) 'living theatre', etc. (2) all sport (3) cinema.—Examples.

1953. MR R. A. BUTLER (*a*) exempted amateur sport; (*b*) amended law on 'amateur drama'—admitted a paid instructor, producer, manager, or adviser (free of tax) to an amateur dramatic production—but firmly resisted a paid conductor, or 'member of the orchestra'; and (*c*) on same day, exempted cricket, which may be played entirely by professionals—Claims of other sports lengthily debated.

The 12 (or 13) Exemptions—highly entertaining.

1954. MR R. A. BUTLER made a slight reduction everywhere.

1955. Manifesto by Theatres Entertainment Tax Committee—As predicted at Academy Banquet, 1953, Labour Party, at General Election, declared for abolition of tax on sport and theatre.

V. THE BATTLE OF 1956 *page* 113

[1] Fortieth anniversary of collection of tax, 15 May 1916. Hopes high—new Chancellor MR HAROLD MACMILLAN—man of ideas and drive—'If anyone can teach the Treasury new tricks . . .', etc. —358 Members had signed Motion for reduction or abolition—Case and organization stronger than ever.

[2] But danger from new and inappropriate quarter—Odd but fascinating correspondence between Arts Council and T.E.T. CO.—Arts Council refuse even moral support to T.E.T. CO.'s cause—Extraordinary reasons:—Tax-abolition on main body

Appendices